T0039285

Untouchable Feelings

Untouchable Feelings

Untouchable Feelings

Tina Jesus

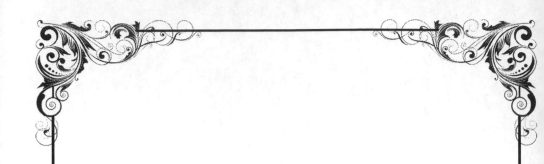

Copyright © 2014 by Tina Jesus.

ISBN: Softcover   978-1-4931-7714-1
               eBook   978-1-4931-7715-8

All rights reserved. No part of this book may be reproduced or transmitted in any form or by any means, electronic or mechanical, including photocopying, recording, or by any information storage and retrieval system, without permission in writing from the copyright owner.

This book was printed in the United States of America.

Rev. date: 02/27/2014

To order additional copies of this book, contact:
Xlibris LLC
1-888-795-4274
www.Xlibris.com
Orders@Xlibris.com
539982

Contents

Introduction

Decent of the holy spirit

Wedding in can-a

Finding of Jesus in the temple

Assumption

Angel Gabriel tells Mary she is the mother of god

Coronation

Scourging of the pillar

—the voices—

Invoking our lady of sorrows, the jattidles of
the exterior cover—Language of—

Archangel language —such words boring, Uriel unvailed—

There's not such as feasts days, although there
is—invoking Our lady in an image—

The play

Between valentine jattidles—Uriel

Burnt roses of
The garden
Thorns of green

Oral sex such a boring word, not such thing—jattidles—devils
Chat in demons crucified by Anthony the great—
Words of gold—the Maddonna—seen in our ladyof Akita—
The black and white image captured in art, not displayed

Uriels reply—

Archangel Raphael—
St Anthony the great saved the soul of the handicapped, similar to
Jattidles Blattidles of dogs put to fight—
Horrible story—Uriel loves him though—not Uriel—a sarcastic
Truthful bitch the author—
"red" the theme—quite the opposite I am, must speak, archangel
Michael my husband—
Pesos the vendor would—mistaken
identity—todo espanol—perhaps
The native tongue—or shall i say or say—unspoken thoughts—
Perhaps, Uriel—I beg—oh uriel—kill for him—a truthful bitch
Though i know—not appreciated—
Xx
Mother and daughter—the virgin and Tina Mary—2014
Go f yourselves.
Final statement and prayer—

Anthony the great—the author invokes—

Xx double double click xx

On the front of untouchable feelings

I'm not an artist, writer; a passion from heaven and
founder of sn ever tree And sandcastle village, My
family, are the archangels, saints, the gem;

Write at the bottom of book,
Visualize a garden of nudity clothing of leaves And thorns
Of roses from the garland of roses beneath st valentine, The
garland of roses are of the little flower Burgundy roses.

(this passage derives from my journey in voices
interacting with demons and Heaven)

Sandcastle village in the center of the cover, A death experience while
valentine Tend to me beneath the ever tree, I said, I'm prepared to
die should the pain Go away, Pulling and tugging on my hand I saw
heaven The little flower opened the door Just sandcastles I saw.
Flower ever.

Jeers to the virgin Mary; visualize images of
thorns and roses Scattered in a garden.
Kattaddoles and jattadoles
Black lace and the owner of two underwear.
Private no more, a scandal of I got,
I did not, all items I once owned
Relatives and friends invited to to view A midtown horror, though
shes a friend I resort to nothing Just my archangels from heaven And
the promises of the rosary Though I am catholic just not catholic.
Valentine my writers pen is in your pocket,

On this cold February morning the first, just before the railroad track sets in, archangels and saints and heaven, hates Satan; The life of a writer, pitter patter of the keyboard the silent typewriter,

Gold for words, just another song to the publisher; my work must be done; the dance jeers romance; in the garden., a writer never tires as sleep sets in her eyes, just one more just one more song of the garden

Blattidles, valentine jeers Uriel,

The romance language continues;

Unexplainable touches, wicked eyes of Uriel and valentine, Such boring language of romance from yesterday; Nudity, to wicked eyes exchange; Dirty language a thing of the past,

Earth and heaven exchange, Tina Mary Jesus,

valentine and Uriel,
Beneath the ever tree, lights are dimmed, the reflection of Therese the flower across the room looking at the virgin, jeers in her eyes the wreath of the archangels, nudity is a beautiful thing, barefoot The love of valentine and Uriel; heaven and earth exchange, On a cold February winter day;

Such repetition, demons I hate

The naked dance in the garden, covered in leaves I envision, a black haired wonder as Uriel patterns of leaves Around the burgundy of roses; valentine on his knees just Xx xx

Unnamed,

Xx Uriel and valentine, xx
The wicked dance of raisins, apples—and jattidles kattodles Xx

February 1st. 2014

8—am, my eyes are tired, the days of normal rest a thing of the past, my eyes penetrating on Uriel, valentine, Mary, Lucy Joseph and Jude against the wall, wreath and the ever tree, fresh snow; spring soon nears, Demonic control is not a joke, spells And curses, waking up sudden movements And resistance a part of the life of demonic control, birds chirping, Songs of nature sung, I guess the garden made it to belville, Of valentine and Uriel. Hate to think after many years of demonic control the voices may be silenced, exercising at 5;30 am, sure different from years ago, Mary I trust in (disturbances of the voices) causing fiction in my brain; working and curing it is a Saturday morning; fighting to stay awake, hail Mary help me, (silence of voices) Torture in my eyes, hush hush and the bird chirps, passing cars The Maddonna availed, final corrections on the book—last night, early morning; Dear Mary, The book is going to be published, the garland of roses; Therese in the background; just a cold day in belville, new jersey; gold and beautiful Your hair of black: Uriel the voices may soon be a thing of the past, brushing My hands on my jattadoles (legs—heaven language) the voices are making me Laugh, still thirty pounds to go, fat girl, I am, size small, medium in juniors Just a nobody, loving the virgin mother of the unnamed, dressed in gold uriel And valentine in the garden, the garland of roses; Hi there Therese, just a torture to loose the extra weight, then again, Valentine, it is only you and heaven I really care about, just carry me through the name calling and bashing, the season of devil and heaven on my side.

Jeerful in early February; oh ever tree, easy, it's, many more names What money power and wealth paid for, the journey of 2014; all for you Maddonna, the Maddonna availed, I'm not sad; unhappy; knowing a paid crime was committed; in a city of "good luck", heaven and the archangels jeerful In the ever tree; gazing upon the saints, fight for me; I'm noting without you

The prayer to the flower,
Oh Therese,
I learned man
Is not an option for the disaster of he'll I trust in you
Therese, After the doors become unlocked I must
not work for cheap, I rely on you heaven.
Understanding why demons were utilized
A mystery, this is just a brain thing, Tina Mary Jesus

February 19th , 2014

Dear —,

An entry of mine," Two candles"—are dim on your dress. Layers Of gold and presents, fill your chair little flower of the bottom visiting her garland of roses the keeper I am, "Marium" I feel So far away regardless of chatting and not chatting, Tequero Mexico Awaiting the publisher, I can't imagine the tears cried, yet st dympha started this, Where is she in heaven, I know the little flower is in heaven
—earth—
I met her—jeers jeers,
Prejudice i face, to minimize my intellect though not reflected On " early childhoods interoperation, college; Paramus, new Jersey Minimal credits, author I now am, Prayers to the virgin—a deal—as discussed—the computerized chip I once contained, remain still—the archangels instructions, My knowledge derives from the archangels—a truthful story—what other alternative do I have other than—to labor in racism employed By you, the only chance of survival I have—as I walk in hate,

Many things have changed, my resume—attorneys assistant—Hire me, the apartment jattidles Blattidles— some addition to Boring language time ago,

Tina Mary, writer—author—visual artist

Not much time I have, as the wealthy and racism is on my foot step—As an owner—my race—everything—Our relationship together based on the virgin Mary—

Start date, immediately—medical I decline, dental accepted Apartment—in the package—overtime, never an issue—

Yes, I accept—based on racism prejudice hate— knowledge Of a resume still in tact,

Jattidkes Blattidles,

Tina Mary Jesus,

"Archangels dictionary"
"Heaven language"

Jatiddles.

Glatiddles.

Blatiddles.

Double click double click

Tap tap.

Pause pause.

Just just.

Boring twang click click

Klattadles Klattadles

Rhythm rhythm Twice

detox detox twice

Flatiddles

Ratilledes

Yatiddles

Matiddles

Platiddles

Tatiddles

Click click

Etliddles

Satiddles

Datiddles

Tatiddles

Batiddles

Detiddles

Jutiddles

Archangel language is a language only known to heaven, while on earth, all archangels must make a heaven connection; No one on earth understands their language other than the keeper of the ever tree;

Only Uriel has a birthday, (jeers) January 23rd, The others weren't given jeers,

A St. valentine classic

Forgotten memories,

A neck bite
Just a wet curl on my neck
Falling in love seems never
My language
To you might I ever
A fairy tale romance
Of yesterday
Night to fall in the
Car in the dark alley
I thought of a woman
Not far away
Apology accepted
I'm you
A writer
St valentines princess

Must I say to you
What color was your beard
And robe of red
I danced for you
Such romance in my ears

St valentine; I chat with you;
A love story of the
Missing song

The song of the season
I must admire you again

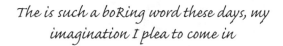

The is such a boRing word these days, my
imagination I plea to come in

Romance language

I brought you roses
Yesterday,

Have you looked
At the red lipstick
Such beauty,

Romance language between
You and I
St valentine

I must go to bed
Hopefully I am not wet

A blood kiss to a friend of yours
I saw the gentle side of him

Might you ever

Incomplete thoughts of a story with a billion
pieces cannot put together

An adoration
Of the untraditional servant

Explicit thoughts
Come raveling in

Tina Jesus

I can't wear the

Night dress
Mesmerized
I must not be undressed
My feet twirl
Not a warm sensation

st. valentine

Reaching for my pillows
Might I wear
Red lipstick

The lips of yours
Might I know you

Twang changed
The climate of snow

I thought I met a fellow
Later on the field
Might I
Love the lace of black underwear

Love notes and chocolate
The vail of the virgin
Pitter patter of the rain
Missing the snow

Have you heard the love
Of the Hebrew goddess
Exchanges; of a young couple

In the meadow
St valentine, might I love
I would never hurt another
Lace underwear soon to
Be the story

Meet me by gate 22
I'll be there at ten
St valentine

Oh the kiss
I never felt
Roses are for the loves
Of yesterday meeting tomorrow

An introduction of your velvet attire
Yellow in the background
His beard of roses
Quite a story of the
Love disciple

Getting to know you
I hope I never sin
The messages quite quaint

Lace stockings,
Might I love you
Romance of two flying doves

Their destination of gold
Quivers of a future
The love of your eyes
St valentine

An xo xo moment

Surprises of intrigue
On the frosted window
Cafe on the board walk

An exchange proposal
Ahh that can't be the case
Heard in the rainstorm

Pink flowers
Under the balcony
I saw the vail

Her beauty of the
Angel,
You must have been playing with me.

The sandcastle of the
Little flower
A castle somewhere

The relics of the little flower
In the garden of the archangels
And the time of exchanges
In the tunnel.

Archangel Gabriel
To the rescue
Some might say
Might might
I dare not ask
Got lost for a second
I'm back

Tokens of Marium
And her vail
Might you remember the gem
The misty rain
Under the sun
I thought of a kiss
And a pony tale

St Jude said
Lost for words
In the states
Have you met the ever tree

Stars for breakfast
Somewhere in the cloud
A name not known

Clouds were named
A passionate kiss
Under the railroad track

The barefoot story

Archangel Michael destroy
Satan from my world.

I digested the gem

Nothing makes sense in some words, just endless tears; to the virgin,

Mary,
Unspoken thoughts,

Allah

I want to know all about you,

Tmj

Beneath the ever tree,
Laying on grass I visualize
Of thee Allah
Just what do you
Look like
Allah
Never go

The leaves of the flowers bloom
On autumn:s door
Fresh brown leaves
Allah has the future
I'm in your hands.

The nativity
Of blue,
The Christmas song
A boy born
Just a wish away

Allah vs Satan

say the words he was defeated,

Angelic eyes

The laughter sets in as the day progresses, my life is in your hands
Marium; The love of the fairy tale bride A wicked imagination Of
sexy meets the archangels Of heaven The coast of the boy in china
I found the gem A love kiss of the bride of archangel Michael My
eyes clasped on the lighting Of the black night Of Stary ville

A tune of riddles and raddles a love making secession
Of the tree of gold All a song to her ears

The story now turns

Some things makes sense
The talk of bedroom language
Oh Marium

Forgive me not
A love exchange
Between friends

He was right
Stupid me
The ignorance of childlike rhythm
I lost the coin
Enclosed in the tunnel

The railroad track
Of archangel Michael at the end

I have your ring
It is in my wing

Might you fly with me

There's no coming back
The tune

A song of the orgasms
I felt is tears
Belonging to your vail

I love the title
Might you approach me

A bashful child

The novenas of Catholicism
Her gem

I swallowed the gem

Digested through never to be lost

The love of the virgin in gold
Might I know you better

Closures; negative church talk
I have the gem

A song for you; might I be a little girl Pony tale

Closures; the Hebrew goddess
And the promises.
I hate you Satan

A blood kiss between the archangel Michael and his bride
Might I bite my lips The blood became the lip color

Closures; adore me ever
The sura I say again, Allah I wish I knew you
better Marium; greetings from archangel Michael
A butterfly kiss, to the woman in gold

Many love stories to report, the love of the
Greenery and an apple in my Helmet,

Found; the ever virgin xx

Another day passing, I'm a servant of the virgin; I felt the
passion of Cutting my finger in thought then the final step,

The wedding of archangel Michael and me, did I give you enough
honor My husband, the orgasm was for you; You can handle me
I prefer you than man Until you are ready to let go of my hand

Xo my hands cold closures.

Dearest mother;

Your vail

I can't stop chatting, the love I have for you and your vail;

Marium;
No one might have you, never permit the devil from
taking you and your gem Away from me,

Closures infant of Prague.

The lonely star sets in; the devil unveil;
crushed by by mother and her vail

Dearest Marium; cry blood to the unnamed, demonic control xx

Archangel Raphael and valentine

*Snow is in the air, her vail and pink roses for her face, darkest
brown hair, and flowers on her body, archangel Raphael
Mary to many not known, I hate Satan, his image beneath
the virgins feet, Radiance of sun on her skin, the love of tears
of gold, Burgundy roses, thorns on the ground In a garden of
roses and the serpent beneath her feet, the silent type writer—
archangels in love with her, her gem and face of pink roses;*

*Time and time ago, once upon a time; a thing of the
past, I must Valentine in black lace and knees bent
on her image, dearest Mary Leave me never.*

Duet of valentine and tina to the virgin Mary

Xx archangel Raphael: healer and valentine romance

*Spring in the air of snow,
Dark blue sky of the stars I named
A pillow under the ever tree,*

Ever tree—the sandcastle on earth for heaven. Tmj 2014

Archangel Uriel

My you're looking
Beautiful
Your hair and dress of gold
A thousand words I might say
Instead
Just
I love your dress
Not shoes as I
The love Allah I found
Beauty poured in my pen
Thoughts of you
Might I wear your dress?
I love the gold,

Tmj
Closures; fancy ribbon

Might you enjoy my company, just by myself
until thee says The shoes must be worn

Fancy stockings i can't get enough of
An empty jewel box
Just the coins I left
From tequero
Mexico

Closures; pouted beauty

Archangel Uriel,

my, one must say; how beautiful you are; The gold
dress, and cosmetics, though; chuckles utilizing Wnd
kwttwddwles wnd dattidles jattidles Archangels; your
language of tongues, is a part of kwttwddwles.

I invoke you, this second archangel Uriel, in my brain Leave me
never, the love of heaven Just another love bite, and perfume

Shall we bake an archangel cookie together

Just blazzinkles blazzinkles, and potato pancakes And apple sauce
Such boring language I love you ever archangel Uriel Beauty and gold

Not shoes, neither sock,

Saint lucy
Have I forgotten you; then again we haven't met,

Saint Joseph;

Marium in jeerful twang celebrated in the year
2014, aren't you jeerful of the Maddonna;

The love kiss of archangel michael, bitter passion
and love On his wing, not as imagined of filth; just
just That is valentines romance, within;

Might might I
And hail Mary
Such a good catholic girl
Xx.

Twang and twang, jeers valentine of romance and neck bites

In the garden, I love being
Not as eve
The apple
I hate you Satan

Love archangel michael and Uriel

Valentine and tina,

Kisses of perfume
Burgundy roses
Beneath the rail road track

A thousand thoughts ago
Just jeers and jeers to romance
In nudity of the garden
Raisins and tic tic tic
Of the silent typewriter;
Little flower
And your wool coat,
Don't forget Jesus,
Mary is pleased to have flower

Roses and burgundy roses
Wicked passion of heaven

Days spent on a silent typewriter
Just pitter patter of rain
Sounds of valentine
Under the railroad track,

Archangels from heaven are you playing in everything

St Michael
St Gabriel
St Uriel
St Raphael

Travel in my head,,,,

Are you dancing and I don't see you
I might never see the past life
I might never know
Yesterday
Prepared future life
Replacing the archangels of heaven
On earth in my apartment

A gemstone
Touches of lotion
Makes a present
Perfumes of my flower
Buried the tricks
Of the past
Play with the itch again
I'm replacing
Replacing romance language,

A fun story of the railroad track; Tmj

Play with me archangels from heaven
Whisper in my ears
The story of the railroad track
A favorite love song of mine

Closures witches and warlocks reunite
Were together the archangels in heaven
A treasure chest
Opened what a delight
Xx xx

Closures: Tmj visual artist and writer, 2014

A silent wish
To the Maddonna
The beauty of tears in gold
Your rosary
Is my gem
Though I cannot say
My world is yours
The virgin
And my womb belongs on to you;

Time has passed; another winter day gone, such romance In
skin not bathed Enjoying the creation Of mankind In bare skin
Boring language This story must be perfect I met you sometime
ago Tosseled hair A dream Not bathed The sexy of beauty And
romance language., There's no feeling As enjoying A waist of gold

Tmj moment

As part of the Maddonna, Sandcastle village

Awaiting cures, from archangels and heaven, you are all
that I have, who What unwanted voices archangels linger
in my brain; Why do the pursue my ruin with my dental,
weight, education and overall Ability to have life again,
separated I am from (impromptu) such intimidation Used
by the spiritually gifted, in all body parts and brain:
They own everything, control everything, archangels
destroy and make me better as I wait on cures from,
heaven; are they really, people; or savages

Xx I am a servant and writer of the virgin, why must
they continue to threat With cruelty, wasn't it enough
what was done in the past, while employed;

My tears of gold Mary, fix everything without me asking, the
world labels me as crazy, then again; why would I go to a hospital
or any place while terror And torture lingers from the wealthy,

I await on you archangel, michael;
Never to rely on Satan, torture with pain and shame the savages
That pursue my ruin, this must stop, now Those are my concerns,
ever tree, help form heaven and miracles and miracles

"composed under demonic control" release me from their
tyranny, give me my life back, Tina Mary Jesus

Dear new York,

If you only knew, you would not judge,

Awaiting the editor

Dearest Marium

As I thought and laughed
The days and nights spending with you
Love on the pillow
Of angels

Xxx interruption if a million demons xxx

Dearest Marium

All music to your ears
As I danced earlier
To your sons birth
Just a few days old
I thought
The past life is done
Upon the midnight clear
Just boring language
Childlike twang
A curse of the profit
There's just you Marium
Listening to the taunts and twang of
Money power and wealth
The past life I had
A million voices
To kill my brain
The past life I cry Marium destroy

Never to return
Upon invitation only
A private prayer of the writer
Not good enough for publication
Just you Marium
And I the promises of your gem

Xx awaiting you to rescue me from the past
life And invasion of the past life xx

Xx a forced reaction from demons, xx

Awaiting your miracles, ever virgin

Might you know
What money power and wealth can do,

Xx

Barefoot

This piece on walking around barefoot is in my devotion to the
virgin Mary, the place belville, new jersey; in an apartment;
the body Is the highlight of twang, Sugar in my mouth, the
wrong words expressed to many ears listening, not truthful
when sugar is consumed; a just for entertainment thing; words
exchanged back and forth to cause Anger and frustration;

Such a bore discussing demons, I must be a good girl all
over again, The life of the untraditional servant, being
watched, listened On erroneous lies and rumors; lies; the
devils story to man; Her beauty the Maddonna, felt in my
bones; a cold night in late January; Tina Mary Jesus

Dear lady; your vail,

Have you seen her song, like a prayer; passion in the blood—
and the knife used to cut her hands—can feel the same
passion—months ago—In the midst of a million voices—
biting on my lips—passion of heaven—while he'll was
poison; my name happens to be Mary. Thinking of giving
blood and giving pricked fingers to archangel Michael,

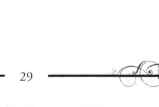

Feeling
The passion of heaven; as a love making secession to heaven.
Passion of a romance kiss; being drawn away; one speculate;
I dare not question today. revealed in passion.
Just a heated moment in heaven., sultry, seductive and
passionate.; I'm black lace, in my writing and everyday life.

TMJ

Barefoot as the pictures i saw
There you are on many
Apparitions
Just barefoot
Oh just love me as I am
The untraditional servant

Bed time stories, The Ever-tree beneath the ocean

Little flower and Jesus beneath the ocean, there to have found a star After riding in the bumper car, the star, huge, a dark blue of a shape notbof a star, amazed at the size both looked attach other and and jeers (and and said in mazal tov) jeers replaced by mazal tov, Treasures in the star of David, an explosive of dradel cookies, games, candles, Joan of arch, the virgin, and the release of, doves and, garland of roses, the Torah and a temple, all in jeers of chanaukah, beneath the ocean,

Blazzinkles blazzinkles and latkahas blattadankles
To Jesus and the little flower Both reading the torah
Beneath the ocean Of fish and hidden treasures

Away in the bumper car,
Candles as headlights for the bumper cars The
nutcracker As an apostle Little flower drives the car
Jesus jeers and jeers Out the doors are opened

A tunnel of a mysterious wonder
Gems gems gems gems
Our lady of the rosary
Reads the Torah
Beneath the ocean
As Jesus and flower
On their hands and knees

I didn't mean to stray away to the temple,

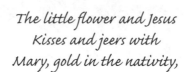

The little flower and Jesus
Kisses and jeers with
Mary, gold in the nativity,

A Tmj tribute of the rosary and Torah,
2014
The gem,

Page decorated with stars of blue and gold, Mary she's gold.

*Laying asleep, The archangel Gabriel appears, watching the
little flower and Jesus in the bumper car, there to have left
apples, not sauce, he reminds the two, ever tree on earth remain
on a diet, Blattadles says flower, Jesus and Mary have apples
on their way back to earth, little flower skips the apples, candy
cane in her pockets, hush hush A secret — no one knows,*

*Bumper car, of gold, the two, little flower and Jesus drives Watching
the star of David beneath the ocean, a dolphin knocks on the door,
Jesus opens the door, I'm the jatizzles jatizzles Of the ocean; little
flower, gives the dolphin a candy cane, from her pocket, the left
pocket on her dress, the dolphin eats the candy cane, only to have
turned into a blattaddles before their eyes, Blattidles in heaven
language — a color no one has seen on earth, The dolphin said
to the two, this happens Blattidles, only in jeers Of jeers, I chat
your, earth and heaven language, Little flower and Jesus, invites,
the dolphin for a drive; all three Began chatting, Jesus, tells the
dolphin, why not drive the bumper car, The dolphin excited,
starts driving as, little flower and Jesus, sits in the Back seat of the
car, the dolphin tells the two a story about, a gem he swallowed,
Jesus and flower astonished, how do you know about the gem?*

Dolphin replied, a beautiful pearl became whole one day turned into a princess And gave gems to the ocean and the oceans families, both Jesus and flower Shows their gems to the dolphin, the virgin was in the ocean before we Came beneath, she's gold dolphin, the princess; Uriel appears as the dolphin drives, adorned in her gold dress, a basket of jeers for the chanaukah Celebration, dolphin, flower, jesus, Uriel, Gabriel the dancer, have a dance Beneath the ocean overlooking the star of David, the virgin, in a blue vail, her body not seen, appears near the star of David, underneath the ocean of jeers. All jeers on uriels day, January 28 Th. Earth and heaven exchange. Dradel cookies handed out, in jeers on uriels day.,

Dolphin and Uriel, this is for valentines collecton not this book The writer of Marium, laying semi nudity, it is a beautiful Thing, the relics of st. valentine beneath the ocean, The relics of the little flower, overlooking the ocean Both kiss, sounds of burgundy roses and crimsons Angels, archangels in the ever tree, Marium might i never believe Nudity and thoughts make my love song Just the beauty of your vail, then again, the writer within Explodes in the ocean of tears, the words must be perfect Of scenery and words of gold to capture the moment of Valentine Marium, the jeers of valentine your beauty is greater than Nudity of Nipples and Uriel A love language of gattudles and Blattadles., Funny story and thoughts and thoughts ago, Relics and crimsons, beneath the ocean in a garden Of thorns and burgundy roses.

Chocolate I didn't find beneath the ocean that is, Black lace and burgundy lipstick The thorns never pricked St valentine in the garden with thorns on the Ground Never pricked

Thorns beneath my feet, I dream of him, St valentine that is, Robes of burgundy. The roses I saw as I slept His gold crown And beard, reminds me of a friend I once knew Lover he's mine, more than a friend St valentine the roses I caught Lover and wine might do the trick Dancing with you in my dreams Nudity is just a Uriel thing Beautiful as I have said St valentine, must I keep saying your name Just boring, Lovers, in words, exchanges of Gold, perfume., buttons; Uriel., my burgundy romance.

Uriel and dolphin

A dance beneath the ever tree
In the ocean
Uriel in her gold gown
The night dark, only the lights she's holding Lights the ocean with gold Uriel and dolphin dances in the ocean Kawatazolles and Uriel Beneath the ocean, In the midst of jeers; Jesus and flower
Invisible kisses To Mary
Her jewelry hidden in the vail
Jeers for flower and Uriel

Not a part of bed time story

The tic tic of the silent typewriter Far cry from the typewriter I saw in Mexico city The tic tic of the keys Interactions with the voices; a trial before a trial All facts gathered together, the judge hearing the messages back and forth On a journey, on the past on a life As I look at the garland of roses And the virgin The ever tree hasn't looked it's best since last November Questions back and forth Nobody rings the radio And and tic tic of the typewriter, All information given to local leaders And power people of power Assuring the closure of doors Before a trial, In the midst, spiritually gifted Ruined my brain and life, gathered twang of Past persons, not been in contact with for years, the former friend, chief of the journey and a religion i didn't know anything about Such boring writing Not my favorite piece The judge and people of power heard, to greet Before hand Without the archangels, though they tried to Cheat me out of the virgin and the saints, Archangels, family, the only family I know The ever tree would have never been Without the rich and money to pay Little flower the past life, Is nothing in comparison as working for the virgin As writer and finding her in pain Tears and concentration Problems Created by a man I gave, Just you virgin and my newest family Can handle this, Who is guilty, not I, i rely on the Archangels that are from heaven I'm truthful and have never lied to a judge, Missing that part of past life, It is wrenching feeling Waiting to testify, One cannot describe, waiting on the judge Questions going back and forth, Just an experience, interactions Just civil to all, regardless of their Problem, That is just past life—archangels What do you think and the virgin and saints Of my future, support by you my family My family—the gem, the saints, I rely on you, I'm nicer these days With my tic tic typewriter, The interaction with Satan at times Heaven all the time, Just signal graces from the virgin Mary Learning about religion finding god Wanting to speak in tongues, Finding st. Jude Taking decisions Becoming baptized in a catholic church Then then just not church as much Archangels, saints, and heaven Finding other channels to god Wanting to know god Walking in doors where both Satan And god is present, demons linger And cling to souls for reasons i don't know I'm a very very very happy to find home And and six hour Saturday's, The archangels and saints, Heaven is a place of sandcastles, and no conclusions Of whose who, I rely on you ever virgin, as writer for you and heaven.

(silent prayer)

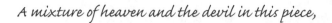

A mixture of heaven and the devil in this piece,

oh archangels from heaven,

A heartfelt apology to my archangels and saints and the virgin Mary,
Nothing I am without you, my writing my work, Belongs to heaven,

Xx I'm no attorney, the voice behind writing, leads to poor
conclusions, I have much to learn, what do you think,
Archangels, I need everything from heaven, (interaction
with a voice, what is the next chapter about?)

Dearest Marium

I fight to love you more,
The serpent beneath your feet
Barefoot as I am
Just what does the colors represent?
I hate Satan and demons
How might you
Help me, I hate interactions with demons Might your medal
be on my heart As dumb as I am Then again your vail, and
your black and white Picture, I hate Satan Keep Satan away
from me, Such boring words Can't find the right words to love
you with The authors pen and hail mary hail Mary Who sends
demons to harm me Might archangel Michael chase the demons
away Thoughts and an energy, where does that derive?
I can't be apart of that, that's past life, I hate demons;
Looking at picture of an authors, book, the serpent beneath
Lays past life, I rely on you, The writers pen, (disturbance
from demons) loss of concentration on my flow of thoughts,

No one can answer my questions, just you Mary?
I rely on you for the best scenario of my future and closures to all
people of Satan, unless the archangels prepare me to handle otherwise,

I don't want anything to do with the color game, I don't know
who They are, what they represent, and why and what possessed
me to give as much as I did, dearest mary, I am apart from the
past life; I don't know who they are, just don't know; if prejudice
and race; had to do with this, I know after my service with
you; no sexuality, such controlled twang of not my own Dear
Mary; my future and life is in your hands not Satan, I don't
know who he is or was, just fix things, afraid to ask of many
things; when where and how Mary I rely on you; for everything;
while having nobody and nothing; just you ever virgin;

Sounds of childish twang; the tone of the voice of the author;

Just barefoot beneath
The ever tree,
Awaiting on my miracles
From heaven,

Being in heaven, just being in heaven., there is no other feeling,
erroneous Lies and rumors.; the railroad track I have not seen;
the past life just so Can't get rid of them, I just await on you,
pause; interaction with the voices Brief silence; in belville; New
Jersey, demons and a crime for money: dearest Marium; I desire
from you only you; knowing who you are; the presence of a man
in the apartment, silence fury, on men and women; just why?
Glee and joy of cheers in the hands of the rich and wicked;
Marium identify these people; and weigh in; an open mind,

can't say much; just history in the make of the Maddonna,
Checking in with the publisher "I am now an author", Just
awaiting on my books, corrections that should have been made;
just just And tap tap, Fat as I am, the love; of the virgin; and
the archangels twang; the music of Christmas silence the room,

Pause in the stained lip,

What exactly do I desire oh virgin, I don't know; just
and just, As I await on you longing as—a husband
goes to sea for fish., I'm longing for you to help me ever
virgin, the brain activity of the silent Typewriter,

Before we met

The curl on my neck,

I never knew you.

Curled up in a position, the blanket is not warm enough;
who am I to love a Woman so filled with god,

The scandal ever of opinions, I rest my thoughts In your arms I rest

I found love in you;

I rely only in you not in "god".

Xx xx closures xx xx the roses

Demons cannot unravel the hidden ever,

Might that be my
Wish archangel Michael

Xo

The untouched sex
My I wish there was another word,
I miss the coffee shop
Though things are not ignored
My love for the virgin
Is in her vail;

Xx the ever kiss xx

Blue shorts girl

Valentine and Uriel debuts
In untouchable feelings
Orgasm chic, the name is silent.

Uriel of gold, Lucy, the virgin, jude, Joseph

Jeerful of valentine and Uriel in the garden, orgasm
chic Of a woman interaction, in the garden Of Adam
and eve meeting god, Satan tempts, she curses him
In modern times; I hate you Satan;

Uriel dances in the garden as valentine is
her lover, Untouchable feelings;

Earth and heaven exchange,
St Anthony the great, Blue shorts girl,

Little flower, Jesus, Gabriel, Raphael, Michael, dressed in Leaves,

Fruits on Uriel and valentine, Nudity is a beautiful
thing, Of burgundy roses, thorns and burnt roses

In my first book, much hateful words; however "I prayed" to
the virgin and her gem, jeerful of archangels and saints;

The book the maddonna is Not just senseless words, words of
gold a reflection of the virgin and tears finding heaven,

I clasped my hands
Recitation of
Hail mary full of grace the lord is with Thee

Xx I refer to kill as Satan in my brain interaction of the voices xx
Change of thoughts, hail Mary full of grace; St Anthony the great
I invoke you, defeat Satan from friends and family; Silent apology;
found in orgasm chic, nudity such a beautiful thing, Oh mother
I just can't understand; many things Your vail, Dearest Mary

Jeerful as my mother, abandoning all family and only clinging
To you and the archangels and saints Jattadles jattadles
jattadles Earth and heaven exchange, Tmj 2014

My book, the Maddonna, a trip to a holy site for a
cure from being trapped in a million voices.
Xx jattadles jattadles—the ever tree, my present to thee, Tmj 2014
Final page,

Burgundy roses, St valentine

Days missed, I'm dreaming, of his robe, smiled looking to the
garden; fresh thorns; yet he'll never realize how my scent made
it to his robe; He must know the scent of a womb on his robe x
not just perfume A scent of burgundy roses of my womb let on
his robe, just a secret I cannot tell; heated passion; of his robe, I
must not call him st valentine Finding a new name; my womb
to his robe, Fresh picked roses and thorns on his fingers I'll kiss
each one and accept Im not eve; the thorns of roses on his robe
Not exactly sure how the scented womb got there.walking around
the garden on a naked body; nudity is not a sin; my womb on his
robe the scent at least I made it to his robe; roses and tears of eve;
the scent what must he say Burning hot; my won to his robe;

Continued to st valentine
Romance without being touched.

Dearest,

Romance without being touched, a burning sensation to his robe,
falling Asleep; the lover of passion; I'll make love to him again.
Fresh snow on a January night; just white snow;
untouched Fresh snow on a January night; pause for a
moment; Not on the story; the air of January snow.
Just untouched.

St valentine on fresh roses and pricked fingers, I fell asleep
Your robe I didn't undress; I must fall asleep again, My lover
and romance, the darkened womb of his lover On his robe.

Lovers come to his robe not scent as I, the air of snow today in the garden; eve; nudity from the lovers voice; nudity a beautiful thing; renaming female and male body's to names of just just; just say to you st. valentine it is just just, to everything on a body I wore your velvet robe, just the garden and eve., I'm not, I'm not eve, black lace, god I must have you back, the virgin Now a part of the story; I love you god; nudity is a beautiful thing I must tell the story of the virgin saving my life, Marium the Hebrew Beauty, just barefoot and pink roses of beauty, sounds complicated It is not; said in twang; of black lace. I heard you god, nothing From Satan; just mariums beauty and her gifts; I'm her servant of black lace; just just; my language of lust; st. valentine twang, His robe and knowing him; his eyes; his hair; of romance spending Time with him. Lovers of winters nest finding him on romance in snow.

Dearest ever virgin; pouted lips and black lace; awaiting
your cure as Writer and servant of yours.
Xx thanks for "chats" with "god"
Xx Tina

Where shall I start, the love of st valentine; his
eyes brings surprises This morning as I looked at his
face; sudden shock of my love for his robe.
Handsome, to say the least; his robe so much in love with, my words
are of gold to his smile as the sun peaks in on a cold January day;
the garden of Adam and eve; eve just love her name (,interaction
with "god) (distraction of Satan) the garden and a naked woman
a lover of st. valentines; She pauses and laughs, such nudity I love,
oh, "god", I desire a part of your kingdom permanently; now that I'm
chatting with you; the distraction of demons) I fought for you "god";
back to eve; my position is clear The virgin, my name to her Marium;

chats chats and archangels from heaven Such boring twang of; (a childish girl) that scenario can be changed, the demons has their hands; can't really say they have their hands on my brain (I heard from you; sitting in a person I once was, grandma attire; there You said to me; many things; of a telephone book and separation) chats away I'm now your friend; the archangels and saints; the virgin; all agree.; you're Giving me everything for my love for your kingdom) I hate Satan;, Chats away I'm now your friend, a relationship; no one knows you; I'm Chats chats with you; god might you destroy demons; your son enjoying His birthday on earth) I approach you with, the writers pen; and the archangels, saints and the virgin; your face never to be revealed; we knock at your door; hands and knees bowed; remove Satan and his demons his curses From my life; and brain; god, knock, knock double click of my writers pen (the little flower; might I present you; the servant and writer; of the virgin Mary) st dympha walks in (her endless tears continues) I can't stop crying My tears are gold (she was called names as I) the final miracle is your hands) Heaven and heaven away) boring twang disappears) the unnamed I called you) The Maddonna; Marium and I; need everything from you to destroy Satan.

The virgin Mary makes clear in heaven) she's my writer; her life as job and biblical curses is over; separation from man and woman on her love for me and the gem, the saints and the archangels.

The virgin stays behind; she's my gem; grant our request) xx

Back to st valentine; your scent lingered; on my robe, The beauty of nudity Is just beauty) of black lace and a gem;

Marium; destroy Satan; many thank you's away—my body,
the writers pen And future relationships from heaven; can't be
with anyone on the opposite side,) the story of the garden and
Satan., st valentine distraction of chats Gold to god) his ear.)

Just nudity; as closures; a saint valentines classic—January 2014—

Interaction with the virgin and saints, archangels from heaven; I'm
nothing without you, Just abandonment for a cure for everything, I
never received, neither trust, Interpretations from churches: god; only
you and heaven knows when I'm to return to life; i have everything
with her vail. You must have mercy, and honor for me; for my love
for your chosen daughter; telling the world how powerful She is; I'm
awaiting my miracles and cure) xx such boring language—my
thank you to "god" thank you replaced "by such boring language"
just a chat with You. The pen never stops, Tina Mary Jesus

Red velvet robe I stared at your face; one must know the devil might
trick anothers eye; garden talk of lace and nudity; st valentine the
lover of the Garden, one must say; as the lover of yours, I undressed
your robe; Such boring language of twang and jeers; the writer
within that I am should I Have been afraid of the naked eye
camera; the thorns prick my fingers Roses on the ground stepping
on the flowers of romance, dancing in the garden Romance beneath
your robe, Nudity, black lace and thorns pricked my fingers;

St valentines answers to the lover; such nudity and black lace of
my red velvet robe, I'm in the garden roses of thorns and barefoot,

Barefoot; representing the feet of Marium,

Nudity and the garden, valentine are you near, I miss
sandcastle village, the doors of sandcastles, archangels in my
brain, whose been taking care of me, such boring language,
jattadles jattadales, I would ask, under a different tone I hate
Satan, whose been touching my back, Uriel; forgotten thoughts
Of yesterday; jattadles jattadles; archangel exchange,

Xx xx heaven and sandcastles, I miss those days, I
must not complain; feelings Double click.; archangels
were you in my head, Sandcastles and the little flower
running to open the door, stay on earth flower Xx

The love bites of burgundy roses from the garden,
valentine thorns of green and burgundy roses of, oh
Marium abandon me never, tic tic of burgundy roses

The war must be over by now haven't seen the darkened sky since
December Time spent in heaven, fallen ice; heaven of sandcastles,

A duet of archangels and valentine, a Tina mary song of gold.

Archangel earth and heaven exchange, sexy of black
lace and the silent typewriter, I don't think god bless you
is your language, then again Neither it is mine, just xx
and double click Of earth and heaven exchange,

Roses of valentine in the window; of frosted snow and jattidles
kattodles Of thorns in the garden, burgundy roses, love
bites from valentine, Black lace and thorns of brown.

Xx Marium I trust in you, earth and heaven
exchange, burgundy roses, the love of fancy lace and
black, fancy lace, Valentine, love me ever; Xx xx

Double click and the garden of green thorns,

Valentine under the ever tree of eyes of gold, xx double click
just just Earth —heaven exchange of, the railroad track, of the
missing ticket, Love bites from valentine, xx double click xx

Fallen ice and snow, the jeers of the ever tree,

And and the children listens to the keeper of the ever tree,

Jeers and jeers of the ever tree
Asleep asleep the archangels rest
Five archangels in the ever tree
Music not today
Candy cane and berries
Archangels asleep,
Michael, Gabriel, raphael, Uriel
Jesus and Therese on the top of the ever tree Candy cane and berries
the archangels jeer Mary, the story of Mary; Chosen by the unnamed
Unnamed, I say; for Blattadles Double click twice, Archangel
Gabriel; her friend, He sends her jeers as she lays asleep Tokens of
gems Mary is gold Face of petals roses And and she loves her vail.
Michael protects her,
He hates the devil
Raphael adores her, he's the doctor
Blattaddles Blattadles fallen ice,
Asleep in the ever tree,

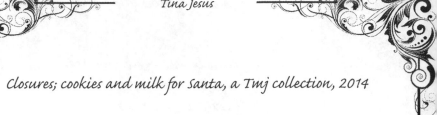

Closures; cookies and milk for Santa, a Tmj collection, 2014

Archangel and heaven exchange,
Sounds of the railroad track
Love of the garden,
Of burnt roses
Kisses without kisses
Xx. Xx
St valentine, is burgundy roses of xx
Not of touches
Just just and eyes of gold
Mary in her pocket
Burgundy roses
Of kisses and touches without touches, Xx xx
Asleep on the ever tree, valentine and Uriel

Uriel,
Of gold
Beauty and a make up station
Of lotions and polish, and and
Such beauty archangel Uriel
Dances in the air
Invisible at times,
Just just
Of a diary
Not told,
Secrets of treasures Mary is uriels friend,

Xx the tale of the missing gem

Archangels in the ever tree
Beads of burgundy roses
The railroad track
Of the ever tree
A train of jattidles and jattidles
Blattidles
Candy cane and berries of archangel Gabriel
Jeerful jeerful of xx and jeers jeers Xx

Ever tree of green tinsels
Relics of the little flower
Beneath the ever tree
I met her in sandcastle village,

Archangels of lace and black
The love of the virgin
In the flowers eyes,

Closures; burgundy roses of the virgin Mary Archangels and Tina a
duet to children, Sandcastle village, Of the flower and heaven,

Xx.

Jeers to the darkest sky, in a fancy lace skirt of black Beneath
the ever tree Jeers of Christmas Xx and sounds of ever tree
garden Jeers of the ever tree Beneath the feet of flower Xx

Raisins and apples
And Uriel
Gold to valentine

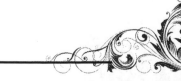

Of nudity in the garden of uncombed hair, Uriel dancing Of thorns below her feet Valentine just the same Dancing Just in effortless movements Archangel michael I bid you near Therese in the words without mention Oh flower burgundy roses I envision between each word Nudity I dare to say not nudity Just another name Tears of gold The eyes of the Maddonna, I said you were "god" Xx.

Jeers of valentine roses burgundy
Thorns are green
Just pricked by
St valentine
Burgundy roses upon her
Raisins
Therese the little flower
Beneath her feet
The missing railroad track
Of rain and lighting

Pitter patter of
Melted ice
Ever tree and sandcastle village,
Station 76547 nj a Tmj collection,

Demonic plague, of jeers and jeers,

Burgundy roses of thorns and love bites Oh valentine Snow is falling Kattsdles jattadles Beneath the ever tree I'll fall for valentine Smells of roses Love of black lace Beneath the ever tree

Ever tree of burnt roses

Scattered through the garden
Valentine is in the garden of the little flower Therese the
reflection of red lights Beneath the ever tree as snow falls
On a cold February day Saints and archangels the love of
Valentine and Uriel Garland of roses Beneath the ever tree

Nudity and and raisins of Uriel
Gold and thorns
Sexy, of black lace and cotton underwear Blattdles
Blattadles jattadles Double click twice Uriel in the garden
Nudity of burgundy Roses, beneath the ever tree

Sandcastle village of hush hush
Sandcastles of towers and and
Girls and, boys jeer
Love of the ever tree
Is ever present
Laughs and jeers
Blattadles Blattadles
Heaven and earth exchange
Jeers of jeers.

Darkened nights of snow and ice
Valentine trots in the ice
Uriel kisses him behind
His neck
Just a bite of a love kiss
Xx xx

Boring words of past life
Oh valentine

Burgundy roses
Xx messages of love
Jeers to archangel Michael

Sexy of the archangels
I haven't read
Jeers upon a time
Archangel Michael had a girlfriend or two Romance of burgundy roses

Black stockings
Of beauty and gold
I must continue valentine
Uriel needs your love

Xx xx messages of jeers
Beneath the ever tree xx

February 5th, 2014

Weather of snow and ice, the snow still falls; the dark sky; Uriel;
is of gold Matches your dress The typewriter of the garland
of roses Uriel beauty of heaven in your eyes Hair of gold:
Valentine

Made a wise choice,
In the garden
Jeers of thorns and dances
In nudity
Of raisins and apples
Jattidles jattidles
Making love
Such boring words
Making love
Eyes connect
Warm exchanges
Of the thorns in the garden
Darkened sky of burgundy roses,

Xx double click xx

Archangels sandcastle village zip code, 76547;!—; Mail to
sandcastle village, Jattadles jattadles Blattadles Blattadles
Earth and heaven exchange, Uriel and valentine,

A Tmj creation of ever tree and sandcastle village, Land
of archangels and saints, the virgin, Jesus and flower,
boyfriend and girl friend, My next book to avail,

Changes

In a shock of a lifetime
The true identity of
The voices
A grim story
For the Islamic princess
Eyes of blood to some
I'll see her one day
By the ever tree
All poised

My husband archangel Michael
Might you deal with the voices
Make me better
I'm writing
Just a dream
Not have much time
Sleepy sets in
Please make me love you more
Just so far away

Might you give your bride
A figure from you
A brain from you
I made tea

Chatting jeers to the archangels and saints, after my service
with Marium; replace my language from past life and jeers
to future life College might ot be an option for the keeper then
again, bar-tending Might Be the silver coin; my hope only in
my family Archangels and saints, the virgin; aren't you jeerful
Marium, your name know to man; I dare to say oh Mary rebuild
my brain; Such a dummy as I am, my archangels might you
rebuild me And give me everything, I hate Satan; Tmj.

Just a vent of words to heaven not "the unnamed"
Little flower, approach the unnamed, isn't he proud I did not
use his name in vain; I hate to ask Mary, for material things,
when heaven is beautiful; the sandcastles and peace;

Falling asleep just wanting death, heaven, jeers for the archangels,

Chatting with demons is not a joke, I struggled to write;
fighting with demons that attempt to gather decisions
and thoughts from Satan; end this satanic reign

Ever virgin, as your writer and the tic tic tic of the silent keyboard
I fell for you Marium, beneath the floor, and just saw your
picture Never have I been lost for words, just never had the time
to Really say; Marium and the archangels you are my future
income; Then past life; what shall you do with past life?

I serve and write for the virgin Mary and the archangels and
saints, the unnamed is aware, sounds of immaturity, not; just
heated passion of heaven in my brain; love and jeers to the
saints, without Them, there's nothing; archangels in the battle
of demons Satan attempt to steal you for bad intentions; then

again; this can't be; I hate Satan, help me ever, I want my brain
back, more creative than ever. Silent prayer; the immaturity
in the journey Represent: heated passion of heaven,

Silence in small potatoes

Oh valentine i strayed away
Nudity is such a beautiful thing
I'm your lover pause and silent prayers Such boring language of
yesterday The eye of the Maddonna Just hail lady help me,

Your writer and lover of valentine

Then again Mary, Jesus and flower and a kiss,
Little flower, just you Mary— Tmj

Demonic control is painful, walking through the streets of new
York, traveling to Mexico city and back, floral park new York,
hearing voices and instructions, writing letters and letters asking for
assistance, a woman; the virgin Mary; helped; I trust in the virgin
Barefoot as she, just the archangels and saints I want in my brain
And the virgin; sounds of immaturity twang, not, the archangels
Were my brain and my instructors; this is not ADHD neither s
diagnosed matter; I have had the ability to function just by Good
judgment, archangels I'm back home, I must remain; destroy
Shall I be separated from you.; a duet of Uriel and tina,

Dearest archangels,
Harsh criticisms, just fix everything, silent prayers,

There my world, my archangels, I found them in
love not for wealth, the gem, Words of gold,

Archangels from heaven; rebuild my brain,

Just a passionate kiss in heaven beneath the ever tree,
I abandoned everyone for you archangels; I just need
everything from you and your words of gold Marium,

A silent tear

That met her vail
, never found your beauty
Ever virgin
Perhaps
Just, your gown of darkest blue

Closures; valentine, archangel Michael and tina,

The sounds of rain, I found heaven by myself, wouldn't separating
in the sandcastle; a beautiful sleep; ever virgin there's knowing
you based on facts of past lovers of yours, then there's knowing you
By hearing from you Your vail,

Archangel Gabriel, chats with valentine and sex, sex
such boring name; Uriel replaces sex; the goddess;

Moonlight kisses
Beneath the sun
Have we met by the rail road track
Valentine, I undressed you

Am I to say; I love you ever
Jeers and jeers

A dancer within,

Valentine, I'm back having to stray out of the garden, Apple
bites, it wasn't you valentine; my love must come from
Heaven, oh valentine, just lust and beneath the blanket,
The story of hidden love and bumper cars in an ever tree.
There, belville new jersey, and exchanges in
midtown and and Many other places

I must be in the garden again, then again just the unnamed
this time, I hate Satan; Marium beneath your feet

Our lady of the miraculous medal, the snake and
the devil beneath, I'm in your hands ever virgin, the
writer for heaven, pause and silent Prayers;

Creating heaven in the apartment; belville nj The
demons in my brain, replace with heaven

The little flower, bring angels of god in my brain;

Shall I write you a number
Might we play little girl
Your hair so blonde
My wool coat
Just a coat I saw of you
Might you play
The ever tree

St Michael the husband of mine
In heaven
A body guard
Not a typical marriage
Xx xx little flower might you playxxx

The demons replaced by angels from god in my brain

Closures

Dancing for the archangels and saints Marium the
Hebrew; Islamic princess in the background,

The saints, from heaven invisible, in the air.

Not the way, I wanted to start the day; then again being controlled by
demons My thoughts: I love Tmj, virgin most kind, Tmj; that's me,

Closures; archangel Michael.

Tmj, away from the past life and all people of the past;
my eyes pounding feels unreal and firmer, ever virgin

This is my time with you; celebrating your
sons birthday and making you happy

Xx.
The ever tree,

I love you ever virgin, Tmj closures

As the songs of christmas ended,

The archangels hung on the Christmas tree, archangel Michael,
archangel Gabriel archangel Uriel; I love you ever awaiting the
ever virgin promises of the gem and the love I have for her

Closures; the palm tree: i loved that story, and
the pain you felt, Closures; the vail

xx

Forgotten thoughts,

As words pour onto the keyboard, I forgot yesterday;

Shall I forget yesterday
I love you ever, virgin, I'm Tmj.

In the midst of hysteria, the demons distract;

This book;

The case of the missing girl
And the tag of Tmj
My identity

I getting prepared, for no memory of yesterday,

Xx ever virgin xx the unnamed said no one should know anything about me, Grant my wish; closures the rosary. And your love for me,

Ever virgin: Many people know you today; closures gold to ashes.

The witch.

Ever virgin my dying breath of your vail, the
words of music is my love for you,

Ever virgin; your untraditional servants request;
everyone from the past remain The past only by
invention of the archangels and me, Tmj

Tina Mary Jesus, my name and love for you ever virgin

Closures Mexico loves you
The truthful untraditional servant. Xo xo Xx

Burgundy roses of a naked body

Darkest blue sky ever replace once upon a time, such a
bore as my fingers Tic tic tic of the silent typewriter

Dear unnamed,

I love you ever, I'd die not having anything than
to loose my place in the sandcastle village

Xx Never never have I utilized Satan;

Kill for me those that attempt to associate me with Satan,

I hate Satan; I hate Satan. I hate Satan Just waiting in Mary,
unnamed, not on you She is your queen, I'm her writer and
servant Funny story of how we met St dypmha and a real estate
book, forgotten by the wealthy rejected and Loss of friends, kill
for me unnamed; I did not know what the game Was about.
Ever virgin, I love you ever,
Making love with valentine
Oh touch touch touch me
Never stop
Do not let go of me waist as
Pitter patter. Pittter patter of the rain Stopped Nothing more romantic
as being in the dark And jumping over a railroad track Valentine
the love bite I'll never forget Kiss me over Again again and again

Valentine, unnamed, st Jude and the writer
A lover of the virgin Mary.

Dear st valentine

The thoughts keep pouring in

Empty bottles of lotions and oils
I'll lather up
For you
St valentine
Polished toes and stockings.

Tmj

Dear unnamed

An empty thought,

The blood kiss to the archangel Michael Demons force the invasion of her book I love you ever, she's resting Might I send her a pillow From the gem The apostles name written With my Stigmata

Closures

St Anthony the great
And st dympha

Xx

Dearest archangels and saints

That are from heaven, am I to say, I rely on you: defend
me Demons in my vision and brain: I hate demons
rely only on the virgin And the archangels,

I bare the Stigmata of Christ in my brain, a duet
between Friends, st Anthony the great and tina;

Dearest st Anthony,
Who did you rely on while "god" made you suffer with
demons And then became great, I rely on the virgin, I
hate demons, just the sura and Ava Maria, Marium
The Hebrew goddess and the Islamic princess;

The fight of my life, I don't want from Satan; st
Anthony the great, defend me with "everything".

Tina tells the archangels a story,

Jeerful to the dark blue sky, snow, on the ground, Christmas songs
Mary in the back ground; incomplete story, demons invaded

Archangels that are from heaven, I love you ever defend me, such a
tale of lies of the devil, I hate Satan; archangels tale, Combat combat
combat, defeat Satan, never love Satan, I'd die for "god" the unnamed,

One would say "pray for a happy death",
sandcastle village years from now.,

The ever tree, heaven is in midtown and new jersey, little
flower Therese., Archangel michael, ask the unnamed, My
soul belongs to god and the archangels and saints that are
from heaven., writer and servant of the Maddonna.

Tone of excitement, god must intervene on my behalf,
Satan and his messages still remain on television, I hate
Satan, Earth and heaven exchange, tina Mary Jesus,

Living a journey of heaven and resistant of hell, back in the
garden Not what I would love to tell the archangels,

Valentine and Uriel in the garden, archangel Michael, visits
as the virgin, is Mary., my name is Mary., the love of the ever
tree—On my finger tips, night sets in; the heat of spring; the
prophet Created a disaster, sounds of horror, just a joke between
the prophet and I, he can take the joke, forgetting his; millionaire
Friends, then again archangel Michael, ask him; a thing or two;
Sounds of Latin music in the air, the composer unknown;the
reflection of Therese in the corner—black underwear, and a bra
Beneath the ever tree; the virgin as mother; laughing—the demons
distract of past friends,; the doctor, I wonder if she's listening,

I must say
Hail Mary, hail Mary help me,
I'm a writer and servant of yours,

Sounds of Latin in the air, Como estas, Brooklyn, friends
of a company, sorry; silent story, exchanges of Brooklyn,
Astoria New York, wood haven Ontario Closures

Silence in the night,

Valentine, and uriel, the thought of cooking you dinner
then again Take out is best, the archangel Michael might
just just Whisper such boring romance Rich of nudity
in the garden, beneath thorns of burgundy roses.

Pause in silent prayers; archangels Raphael; my brain As
valentine awaits, the devil rampant in many ways Yet
theres, summer in the air near the rail road track,

The devil, laughter of archangel Michael; I gave you to
valentine, Uriel and the lost token of the blue sky in belville.
Just the garden, where is the unnamed
these days, the devil was defeated,

Xx—just just, unnamed and the unknown together xx
Valentine the burgundy roses beneath the leaves of Ava,

Xx
Where are you valentine? Snow and ice again, the tone under
the ever tree of sleeping in the dark and not sleeping, the clues
of television every now and then, demons and their tricks, I hate
Satan Archangel Michael, the ever tree is lit of Jesus birthday, sleep
sets in unspoken thoughts, The threat of Satan, on television; oh
archangel Michael, "not sympathy" detectives in a murder scene,
sounds frightening being alone, then again there are archangels
from heaven in about, Dear unnamed Thanks for granting my
petition Then again st Joseph is imbedded in my heart Patron saint
of, sudden death and calamity, Funny story of the pope giving the
prayer to emperor before battle, Archangels and saints in the garland
of roses, The angels that are from heaven do come when there is
danger On earth for their friends, sounds of immature twang Just
divine Jesus, little flower found you as a girl in a fancy wool coat,
Tina Mary Jesus

Dearest Mary

Chuckles of the past life, almost as a scenario of, the tale of "whose been sleeping in my bed" Marium whose been in my brain Touching my heart, past life might not know me, know me not to know me;

Kattsdles and Jattedles
Earth—heaven exchange, archangels Gabriel
Raphael Michael and Uriel; I invoke you this second
destroy Satan from my writing and brain

Past language of prayers—a reflection on my last book.

Xx your bitch servant xx

Im home, duet between valentine and Uriel. I hate Satan,

Silent personal prayer.

Dearest Mary.

Naked and cured

Walking around in underwear
A bra no less
Expecting miracles and cures from you
Marium
Am I to think
I am crazy
Some might argue this is unreal
Disagree I must
I love you ever
Playing the piano I never did
Although I hear the music in my head
visualize
The pillow I created
Sometime ago
I rest my head
A funny story
The closure
Is not available to man
I await on thee Marium

Xx closures; unspoken words

Dearest st Jude

I desire nothing from Satan and his followers; kill them
dead if they approach me be food, hand exchanges and
cleverness, I rely on you st Jude; I'm just as you

If I had a wish
I d say unnamed
I would die in the little flowers arm now this
second Instead of serving Satan

I reject Satan, the good catholic girl is back Repetition of
nine hail Mary's Nine our fathers And nine glory be's

Pitter patter of the silent typewriter
Just watched the garland of roses
Little flower
I'm ready whenever you are
Tell the unnamed
The saddest story ever

*Unnamed are you proud of me; not a lover of church
just of the Hebrew goddess and the Islamic princess*

*I hate Satan, get out stay out and never return The days of
knife whalings are a thing of the past Know me for who I am
Twice by two prophets I hate Satan and don't want anything
from Satan I m not associated with the color game,*

Archangel michael; destroy for me,

*I'll consider the love bite as a kiss from valentine I'm missing
the unexplainable touches Such a feeling of warmth and
wetness Never I want to rely on you devil I approach you never
Fight for you never, just the rosary Captured by our lady of the
miraculous medal Defeat Satan; closed bible just the gem*

Oh and oh and, Mexico city loves you Mary, your writer and servant.

Tina Mary Jesus.

Dearest st valentine

I'm yours as well, the love of Marium wnd nothingness
led me to you; the archangels are my life; I know you and
the others as friends. I must know more about you;

I want to have my own image of you,

In chats and dances I'll love you more. Many
thoughts come to mind when i stare at you,

Just how did you become st valentine? I'm Tmj, enjoy
the time with me Our friendship to last eternity,

Closures st dympha,

Sitting and staring awaiting a cure in an apartment,
decorated for heaven, just how does it work in heaven?

Closures
St Joseph

There on the ever tree, hung; archangel Gabriel stands
out, I need my miracle My family, many miracles;

Closures archangels from heaven

Allah made an appearance, the savior of
Tmj, I'll introduce you to Allah
In the apt then again, you have met

The sandcastle,

Tina Mary,

Valentines day thoughts
I cross my legs, not seductive, just in black stockings awaiting
Miracles;
St valentine some exchanges

A sexy dress of lace
And perfume on my neck
The perfect shoes
To make a number
Just no lipstick
Sheer lace black preferably
Chocolates
And roses
Hung on the ever tree
St valentine
Our first valentines day together
As music hits my soul
I love you
Such boring words
Cant seem to think of the
Right words
I ll wear the shoes
Not red black
Getting prepared with
You
In my fingers
On my legs
In my attire

Ill fall for you
Not good enough
The words of romance
Fine cheese in an eatery
Perhaps in my kitchen
Time together
I found my date
What might my present be
I love you
Must think of another word
Of sexy black lace
Typical languagen
Said in sultry seductive
Twang
I'll fall for you
The fancy black lace
Dark chocolates
A must,
Girls having fun
Words of love
Just a boring word
Might we begin our friendship
St valentine

Closures; archangel uriel

With your fancy attire and all
Venus the greek goddess
The thoughts are rsingb
Fresh flowers on the
Car
On my bed
This duet must be
Fancy lace stockings

Closures. Heels and wine to avail

Dearest st valentine,

A st valentine classic

The silent typewriter resumes
The red
Lacy dress
I chose black
closures; the banquet of the rose garden

Dearest unnamed

I hate Satan, I hate Satan and anyone connected to Satan, Unnamed, might you know the truth between me and my friends I cannot be cursed anymore because of past life friendships Both moved on in their lives and except one apologized at the end, In an unspoken apology and truth and honesty I want the truth of tea time and ava to come forward and cannot be publicly humiliated any longer because the prophet had a dream To build a church, I'm not connected to my former friend in any way and to be judged By christians politicians on worthless assumptions; is not fair. Unnamed, I have been faithful while children family and Friends started a ridiculous game I thought, satanic, game, used spells on me to make me loose my hair, brain, teeth, gain weight Loss of blood, back problems—all I ever said I rely on the virgin Mary and on heaven, I'm in lace and black; do not know what the color game is. Make a decision now "unnamed" while the rich used prophets to make me loose everything; they had all the money in the world to pay him I refused, even though it was mine. Do not let me be disgraced Or mistaken for a thief, i trust you unnamed. Unnamed, my name for god; Might you know unnamed the true story and today make a decision, I have given everything to past colleagues, friends, and betrayed because of hate. The nation in solidetary of red game and Satan, I am not, then she winked at me; since I'm the looser of the game The friend of therapy, for years approach all these people and really Greet them for me;

I expose my love for you to the world, and want you to be a part of I rely not on you god, the archangels and saints and the virgin Mary. Marium the Hebrew goddess and the Islamic princess;

Dear unnamed

I um promoting Mary the year, 2014, awaiting everything from
her Since I've separated me from nothing; or rather you separated
me From nothing; jeers unnamed, I desire nothing from satan;
Just awaiting Mary, Marium I like to call her. I cannot be abused
labeled mistreated., for laughter; I rely on Mary with just her
spiritual necessities. The earthly possessions; I have never stolen;
Neither cheated in any relationship; dear unnamed my life remain
A mystery I await on Mary, throughout this journey all I spoke
about was Mary; jeers for nothing; he might go today with all of
his belongings, approach everyone on my behalf, I await on Mary.

Tina Mary Jesus.

Dear unnamed,

Everything and nothing seems to be the game for everything I have
Leaders and my ex husbands family apart of the rich and their game,
I resort to Mary and not you; I don't know what the spiritually
gifted did to you or asked you: I don't know you unnamed just some
conversations in the garden; I know Marium the Islamic princess
and the Hebrew goddess; the archangels from past experience; I trust
Mary and her gifts to me in my books, today and forever Having
only the archangels and saints to count on. What an experience
working in a midtown company, then resigning not on my own
a terrifying experience, rescued by the virgin and the archangels
Kill for me unnamed the sources that want to take my archangels
I found them in pain when there was abandonment; not my fault
unnamed; he must treat me as a person and all past life people that
have gotten so much out of me because of kindness and friendship.

Just opened doors matter as to who I am and not
guilty, the writer that I m of the virgin Mary.
Destroy unnamed, I enjoyed speaking with you in the garden, not
the same as testifying, neither being a jeerful assistant to many, just
wrong on decisions and persons she trusted for facts, I made up with
her, now, just awaiting, Marium and the new life, they must not lie
about me I am not mini; don't have a family and awaiting heaven,

The good catholic girl came back the moment Satan questioned
my love for you, my books Jeers the jeers of the virgin and I
work together, the year 2014; united states of America,

Just Mary.

Dearest st Jude

I desire nothing from Satan and his followers; kill them
dead if they approach me be food, hand exchanges and
cleverness, I rely on you st Jude; I'm just as you

If I had a wish
I'd say unnamed
I would die in the little flowers arm now this
second Instead of serving Satan

I reject Satan, the good catholic girl is back Repetition of
nine hail Mary's Nine our fathers And nine glory be's

Pitter patter of the silent typewriter
Just watched the garland of roses
Little flower
I'm ready whenever you are
Tell the unnamed
The saddest story ever

Unnamed are you proud of me; not a lover of church
just of the Hebrew goddess and the Islamic princess

I hate Satan, get out stay out and never return The days of knife whalings are a thing of the past Know me for who I am Twice by two prophets I hate Satan and don't want anything from Satan I m not associated with the color game,

Archangel michael; destroy for me,

I'll consider the love bite as a kiss from valentine I'm missing the unexplainable touches Such a feeling of warmth and wetness Never I want to rely on you devil I approach you never Fight for you never, just the rosary Captured by our lady of the miraculous medal Defeat Satan; closed bible just the gem

Oh and oh and, Mexico city loves you Mary, your writer and servant.

Tina Mary Jesus.

Dearest virgin

Jattidles jattidles jattidles double click for Jesus., earth time,
2014; criticisms and words of the devil through man;
The night mare to end now,
Virgin, do you know what man has done to food, I introduce you and
your gem To earth, Translation out of demonic plague, Blattadles
jattadles Blattadles Repeat hattadles jattadles jattadles, replacing
demonic language, archangel gabriel jattadles Oh virgin, the holy
spirit, the apostles, on my pillow, can't name them Just a memory
thing, said-in twang of. (rhythm) jerrful, The holy spirit upon
my head, saints against my wall, why; st Jude was mistaken, let's
chat; oh how was that so? Said in twang of (rhythm) St Joseph,
the story of my brain The authors plea, must must I (bending my
knees) Bernadette for a second Change of mind, the three children
of Fatima, oh their names, Francisco Jacinta, oh and the other
one, my jeerful jeerful of flower, Xx decent of the holy spirit xx
Interactions the demons, laughter; back to my story, (laughter) oh
virgin most kind, silent prayers; burnt roses on my pillows Scent
of flower, Jeerful on your feast day, our lady of Lourdes, I cannot
create a muddy stream, yet I might imagine, jattidles jattidles—of
muddy waters years ago, Oh Bernadette, drinking water in a small
town I knew, Archangel language—jattidles jattidles—I spoke
in tongue, (jattidles, miracles known to man, after a servant;
Bernadette, jattidles from the virgin, cures been known to earth,

Tina Mary's version of the rosary in words of gold,

Xx holy spirit—xx my thoughts of Satan in my brain
a tug of war to reveal the secrets of heaven, I've come
this far, oh virgin instruct me even more.
Tears of gold, oh virgin,

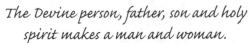

The Devine person, father, son and holy
spirit makes a man and woman.
Gems, a reflection of all, the virgins romance language of archangels
and saints, Candles and the priest i haven't, jeers to heaven on your
anniversary Of our lady of lourdes, creating; archangels, saints,
spoons of drums Dance, your sons birthday in earth language, a
better word or so I thought, jattidles jattidles, archangel language,
the gem in my words of gold, jeers of uncombed hair, dancing;
Therese—I say is Jesus girlfriend. Chats in ordinary language,
(thoughts of the author, Your voice oh virgin, disappear never,)

Creating, imaginary friends, dolls greeting you on your
day, Then again, the tilma I didn't capture; perhaps in
a shopping bag, somewhere tucked away; a token in a
photograph, Our lady of Guadalupe, jeerful in saddness,
the reflection on a book once written, the Maddonna;

Tears of gold, silent prayers; archangels archangels, xx double click,
the keeper of the ever tree—telling earth—my brain was built by
Heaven, jattidles jattidkes jattidles, (said in enthusiasm and jeers)

Dearest virgin, i rely on thee, grant unlimited miracles,
the scent of flower on my pillow; burnt roses, of thorns love
bites, Romance of valentine, Jesus and Therese, oh virgin,
Your vail; archangel Michael, archangels my tears in
the Maddonna On poetry of gold, i trust in thee,

St dypmha, jattidles jattidles—past life, and material
I await on thee, unlimited miracles, virgin.

February 3rd, 2014
Archangels that are from heaven
Defeat Satan

Jattidles and kattoddles kattodles earth and heaven exchange
Demons why must demons be in my brain Ureil i say to you
destroy and kill without death; st Lucy My eyes are in your
platter; childlike twang of hatred of Satan Knowing the thorns
of valentine beneath my feet, I hate Satan, the time spent on a
cold season; Satan is defeated by archangel Michael and Uriel his
bride, the author, changes twaddsnlles and gattadles Blattadles
kattsdles gattadles Gattadles gattadles kattsdles The curse from
archangels michael, Uriel, Raphael and Gabriel ton the devil
from the miraculous medal and vattadles the keeper clings To
the archangels that are from heaven beneath the little flower.

Archangel uriel in the gold dress beneath the garland of roses.

Therese and jesus in the ever tree, jeers on his
birthday, Marium Never thought I would ask you,
jattadles Earth and heaven exchange.

Xx a woman in a million voices xx on a cold
February day, spring And jattadles xx.

Ureil and Michael

February 3rd, 2014
The letter

Spring upon the snow in belville; gazing on the archangels and saints, Knowing the cure and miracles I've been awaiting nears, Trapped with annoying voices, I hate Satan and honor the virgin Mary; dedicating books to her and the rosary.

Rosary, beads of prayers, jeerful; my, time has passed And I am now the untraditional servant of the virgin Mary; a writer And author that developed in an exchange of heaven and earth.

Just the virgin, might secure my future after my time with her and her archangels and saints.

Afraid to really share the extent of the cure, Satan lingers in the air,

Earth language; my resume, on your desk; awaiting a start date from you in your company; I've changed since we met and look forward to being thoroughly trained by you and the others. The salary, I trust in Mary, the virgin, . . . Let me know the start date; There is a glitch, I am trapped in a million voices, very complicated story; the knowledge I have derives from the archangels and saints And a couple of people out there; since the condition has developed I have had much time to understand, the virgin Mary now being my Supervisor, since I am her writer and servant;

Many more things I have to offer, devotion to your business and Learning from scratch; creative, am able to spend hours on a computer, while working with a gun to my head, I am not holding you To over time, just a break and not for cheap,

Tina Mary Jesus, my name changed for symbolic reasons

Heaven is a beautiful place

That loves obnoxious bitches

I saw heaven, in a black laced top

Laying near the ever tree

Archangel michael I love you forever

I saw heaven

The sandcastle

Xo heaven comes for you,

The angels become so attached to you, I made
a home For them An all year Xmas

Happy birthday to Christ

Xx in the evergreen

Getting back to heaven they come for you. The sandcastle A clear
picture I saw, of the sand, I fell in love Such repetitive words

Nikita Mara and the train ride
The blue jeans I never wore

Xo

I have no opinion neither comments on any
anything; the typewriter Is silent,

No thoughts of yesterday
On past friends
Past life

Closures; the stale vocabulary must be done; vocabulary once
used In Christianity;; nothing else to say; Not a part of Satan;
Archangel Michael; I just can't my language to you.

Tina Mary Jesus

I'll listen in from time to time; is this really happening today?
Just words of gold; Mary; your vail.

Blushing this morning when we spoke
I looked at your picture
Heaven loves you Marium
Allah is taking steps in the war
Your face never looked
This rosy; a glow that I have not
Seen

I dare not question
The unnamed Mary is resting
While you watch
Your writers finger tips
Struggle for the perfect thoughts
Months you really are glowing
Just watch
Your friends stop the war
Using your gem.
You're gold,

Dear god
If I missed your voice; I'm sorry; demons and Satan
Religious men and women ruining my brain. The
gem And heaven a time of heaven on earth;

The gem; I belong to Mary; I just never had a
complete Picture of heaven; until the sandcastle; I
approach the archangels and saints Never you;

I hear voices

A present from friends
A cruel trick
I hear voices
I met heaven on the way,
The little flower is my friend
Baby angels are playing in my head
From heaven
Their friendly and cute
Christ's friends
There's so many of them
A sandcastle village

Love Tina

I m better now
Just heaven in my brain
Of baby angels
In sandcastle village

Love
Tina

Sandcastle village, just tons of fun, Of angels and angels from heaven
Their speaking to me I replaced them with bad angels Never to go
away I'll keep them ever They make me laugh sandcastle village
A friend of mine is there Her name The little flower She's precious
to me Give her roses from time to time She loves you very much

Love Tina

She opened the door of the sandcastle
When I was I'll
Filled with love
She ran away
I love the little flower
A day in sandcastle village
Love Tina

Sandcastle village
Just sandcastles of fun
Darkest gray
Of fun
Love tina

Once upon a time
In sandcastle village of
Bumper cars and candy cane for dinner
I sang with angels
I love them ever
Candy cane for dinner
Maybe two or three

The little flower has a friend
A duet together
Babies again
The little flower and the infant Jesus
Pals holding hands

She found her friend in
Belville nj
A town
Of railroad tracks
And busy highways
Positioned on the windows
Invisible to the eye of man
Their friends
Little Therese and baby Jesus
She loved him so
Found him as a child
Both sitting
Exchanging thoughts

Love Tina Mary jesus

January 25th

Jattidles Blattidles, just just to the ever tree,

Tmj 2014. Oh flower, just jeers,

I made it to heaven laughing at earth

Mankind
Thoughts and beliefs
The sandcastle
I'll never forget
Oh heaven
Make it up to me
Just away from
All
Just no one knows
The creation and
It's existence,
I found the sandcastle,

Closures; no one knows who I am,

Dearest Marium

I await on the angels to help, a hater of Satan and his
followers Archangels; are you fierce and bold, do you destroy
for heaven Destroy Satan; now this second Closures Tmj

I hate coming back from the sandcastle
The most peaceful rest;

Tmj

I'm not angry; relieved—
Of really being nice for years

Not upset at a divorce, just working in my books,
spending time with the virgin Mary and heaven, Just
a cure from demons and their wicked schemes.

A classic song of love to st valentine,

The right words I'm looking for
I just can't fall in love now
Painted toes
Time alone
God
I'm sorry for acknowledging Marium first If I had one wish I'd
make up with you I did make up Through Allah For he's god
to some Anger and humiliation might tease my brain Thoughts
of yesterday Peeks in I sing I dance Where is the beginning?
I love you ever st valentine,
This song is much to pretty
To think of your enemies
I'm a lover of yours

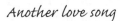

Another love song

If I asked how many lovers have you had What would you say
If I asked you How did you Become st valentine How would
you Answer What would you Say Might I know you more?
Your picture
Is that so
What did you look like,
I saw an image of you
Just what did you look like
I have an imaginary
Lover or two
I ask you to help them
A girl rattled with demonic plagues
The imaginary lover of mine
Plays with my toes
Touches my hair
Wants to go further
I didn't succumb
To self touch
I plea with st Anthony the great
Just who is my imaginary lover
The feelings were pleasing
St Anthony the great did
That happen to you
I've written words
Unafraid to speak
Of unexplainable sensations
I hate the word orgasms
Not a beautiful
Word

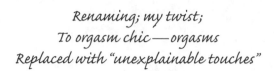

Renaming; my twist;
To orgasm chic — orgasms
Replaced with "unexplainable touches"

A classic love song with — st. valentine on a mid January morning;
planes flying Cold; how many lovers did you have st. valentine?

Laying on the carpet
The fantasy removed
Intrigued by my body
I look at my feet
Twirl my feet
I feel my hair
Laugh by myself
The voices make me laugh
St valentine
Help my imaginary lover of
Unexplainable touches
Just laying on the carpet

Once upon a time
Rent collector; now author

Oh st valentine; perhaps in years to come,
My passion to you to unravel
In words of nudity not seen

Just why many questions, I'll know the answer

I cry for heaven,

Xxx

The love song between st valentine and archangel Uriel

A connection on earth,
Between the two
Her beauty I don't know
Yet I know she's beautiful
St valentine I think of love
Is it wrong to
Love and look at my body
I look at my breasts
I call them potatoes
Looking at my neck
I massage
A passionate exchange
In the shower
Of an imaginary lover,
Unexplainable sensations
Archangel Uriel
Your beauty I desire

A love poem of st valentine, archangel Uriel and
Tmj; a classic

I dare to be an author of many many books, Tmj
Might you love me more,

A love song
Not chocolate and wine
Neither dinner
Just a passionate kiss
With st valentine
A lover that replaced the imaginary lover,

Tmj

I could write a million words
Just a lover
Of my pen
The ink ran dry
I fell in the greenery
A love song to st valentine

How might you be pleased with
My body
I'll dance with my legs in the air
Looking at the picture of the Maddonna
Her vail
Captured
I'm her servant

I dare to be an author
Grant my wish
I'll send you a kiss
I blew you
A picture I took
Looking in a mirror
I saw the story of heaven
She didn't come for me
I saw heaven and my farewell
St valentine

If I sent you
Flowers from my apartment
With the little flower

She has a garland you know
Just casual talk language
I met her close to death
Laying asleep
On the carpet
Just the death that didn't happen
Deep sleep
An archangel of five in an ever tree
Might you accept my roses,
A garland of roses
Making love in unexplainable touches,

The sky today st valentine
Gray and dark
Twirling toes
And nail polish
Of black
Forgetting red
This is my new color
Black
And lace
Falling in love with my figure
My hands so soft
Feet almost the same
My waist sunk in
A description of me
I don't know a description of you
I replace you in the demon
Of love making,
My belly almost flat
Might I await your touch

Or is this our good bye
My brain and thoughts rattle
Away
St valentine might you care?
An exchange between heaven and earth.

Tone; sultry and seductive,,,,

I pout and stare
I'll miss the moment
My own language
A gift to you
Before
Your day
Our romance language
Of love making
Since
The dimmed light of orgasm chic
Replacing words once used
F u replaced
I pout my lips
I hate those words
I have my own love making language
Since orgasm chic

Orgasm chic, now unexplainable touches;

St valentine; bring the pen to my fingers
Just awaiting the publisher
The conversation after love making,
I guess this is what happens after

Heated passion
Replacing the demon of unexplainable
Touches
The story of my polished toes
Shall we conversate just a word I made up
Are you proud of me?
Tell me more about you
I m not just your lover
I want to know more about you
St valentine

The romance language
Of unexplainable feelings
A sensation of twirley toes
Just words that doesn't make sense
We must continue
As a violin played on the fields of
The greenery;

A Tmj moment

Where are you taking me st valentine,
I await for you;
Thanks for taking care of me
I replaced you with st valentine
God lingers in the apartment
I'm amazed at the power
Of st valentine
And unexplainable feelings;

Tmj

*I dare to say
When are you
Stroking me next
What do you feel?
Such boring language,
Not a favorite of mine
The typical f you
Xxx*

A love song of Tmj

I'm not eve

Frosted beard, his majesty in a robe beneath his robe, many
lovers has seen; the tale of st. valentine; his life of lovers;
prisoner to his robe Velvet red, and hands of thorn in his
robe, lovers and friends, of his Just adored his robe; a robe of
gems and rubies, crystals, and diamonds; St valentine, freshly
picked roses and thorns for his lovers; delight in Red velvet
time spent in the; forest of thorns and roses fallen leaves:
Time spent in his robe, a mystery of love and romance within his
robe, The scent of his lover felt in his robe, the scent of roses on his robe;
Fresh fallen roses in a garden; the robe of his lover on a scented bed;
overlooking fresh flowers on a garden of thorns and pricked fingers.
The scent of his lover, on his robe, just fresh pricked roses; and
thorns of a Finger; the lovers scent on his robe; pricked roses
and thorns on his robe The tale of st valentine in a garden
of thorns and roses fresh pricked flowers On the garden.

I fell in love with his beard, walking around naked, I thought of you
last night In my dreams of love making, st. Valentine and your robe,
the fresh pricked roses and thorns, I'll kiss your fingers, just one by
one; thinking of time spent In a garden of thorns, His robe I'm after;
I must get his red velvet robe, the beard on his face I'll take my time
and kiss his beards; daydreaming of roses in the air, the scent of my
fragrance on his robe., the scent he cannot resist certain Of his wishes;
my naked body in his dreams; I'm not eve in the garden Just naked
awaiting Adam; my name I must not tell; my scent on his robe In
his dreams of smaller breasts, and black perfume on my womb, my
scent is on his robe; not exactly sure how the scent became part of
his robe, ahh I do know; I must never tell; just eve in the garden;

and a naked body to hia dreams; The others i dare not question, the black perfume on his beard and red velvet Robe, his dreams of love making; just cannot imagine; scenes of passion My scent on his robe;

Falling on pricked roses, the stems of thorns, where is she, her scent on my robe, cannot describe; just where is she; I'm in the garden of fresh picked roses and fragrances of her womb, thinking of a love bite I want to give her My robe I ll kiss instead; the undressing of her womb is passion to my eyes Grabbing her and kissing her fingers I must, what is in her scent; my robe The velvet must never be taken off; the sounds of lust on her womb; I wish not to be called a saint; her scent of fresh picked roses, and thorn fingers; The lovers of the past; she is not eve, wicked lust; in a garden of fresh Thorns,

The velvet robe, a Tmj love to st. valentine

A virgins tale,

Jattidles battidles

Remember oh most gracious virgin Mary—the love for the unloved Cursed by powerful jattidles not of the eyes of the eyes of the virgin, tears of my eyes—anger virgin—virgin Shall thee remain jattdiles jattidles, silent prayers—I'm not a nun—the untraditional servant as I,

Laughing droplets of Moon kisses

I fell for you.,
Might I take off my hat
How about a kiss
Nah are you too shy
I thought so
I brought a sandwich
We must share,
Water I like best
Tell me about you
The laugh
The chat from last November
I'll run around the garden
Must be home by noon
The song of not st valentine
Mariums tears
Not of blood
Gold gold gold
Her ashes met mother in India
The two became one
I found her
Exclaimed the Maddonna
The two became one
St dympha
Enjoy my present
She's now gold along with the virgin,
I rescued her, forever ever ever she's mine Never
to be mocked, gold replied the virgin,

Sincerely

The iPad is almost done, the story of the author.

No polish

Thoughts of the sexy in your eyes
I'll dress up for you
Perfect gloss
On a sphagetti strap dress
Might I love you
I'll never leave you
Neither cheat
Playing the violin always fun
A typical number of roses
To the Maddonna
Time to fall in love again
Next time I'll wear earrings
Black and white pictures
Not endless song
To my wall

Just fancy stockings Closures Tmj

*Nudity and tasseled hair, Uriel as gold; the
make up station Of lotions and oils;*

*St Jude the relic I question, red and of burgundy rose, just saw
the other day, ever tree is lit the sounds of falling ice and snow;
Nudity beneath the wool coat, of sounds and tone of the author
Just; unspoken thoughts; archangel Michael silent prayers,*

Duet, between Mary and Tina

A Tmj moment,

Nudity for valentine, such boring words the archangels and
saints I remain beneath your feet, knees bent looking upon the
darkest blue of skies, my typical language of a favorite shirt,
sometime ago; Archangels gabriel, Michael, Raphael, Uriel

Your bow today gold as ever
Lights are dim
Beneath the ever tree
We listened to jeers an jeers
Of the magician and a hat
What is the hat?
A ticket of what
What such harsh words
How about
Jatiddles
Archangel gabriel
Kattaddles and kattsdles
The ever tree,
Sandcastle village
Uriel makes a wish
Blow me a kiss
Closures; child like twang, of kisses and tears

Kisses and tears,
Apples and raisins
For breast
Who wants to be a chicken
Not I Uriel
As beautiful as you
The love bite valentine
Kiss me valentine
Sorry, I jumped straight to untouchable Feelings Forgetting the kiss,

Renaming the body parts of a woman
To
Fruits and uriel
Archangels language, jattadales. Jatadalles

Oh uriel,
The mans body,
Must be renamed
Nipples are to be raisins,
Penis, let's just say Uriel
Jattidles,
And kataddales
My valentine, jeers ever, Uriel:

Nudity and burgundy roses
Xx earth and heaven language

Kisses of burgundy roses
Beneath her feet
In the garden of valentine
Mary is her mother,
Chat for me virgin most kind
I trust in you,
Xx and jeers

Earth and heaven exchange — in xx

Valentines jeers beneath the ever tree,

Xx valentine and Uriel,

Cold snow, and a garland of roses.

Xx. Tina Mary Jesus,

Oil and lotions for valentine, from Uriel

Touches in the garden beneath the sun of hot jeers jeers, uriels
Leaves still on the burgundy roses, oh virgin most kind, come to
the garden, valentine of perfume and pure thoughts of raisins,
apples and jattidles kattodles unexplainable touches beneath
the sun of Humid and Blattidles, nudity a beautiful thing,

Valentine and Uriel; dirt becomes fragrance on their
bodies, Nature of the leaves on their skin; hair uncombed,
bare and The unnamed in the laughter of the enemy.;
valentine and Uriel Walked away from Satan,

Their romance of apples and raisins and and kattsdles
kattsdles Sultry and romance, untouched.

valentine classic of Uriel., the virgin, Adam
and eve, The unnamed; Tmj 2014

Oil becomes sweat jeers lotion becomes nature,

Earth and heaven exchange; music of the
pitter patter, beneath the ever tree.;

Our lady of sorrows, I invoke—

In tone of archangel michael my husband,

The media frenzy of cheap

Not, Intervene, you would dare not say to another, public humiliation,

"Our lady of sorrows "

The apology—though I might never see this woman Tears
of gold—in untouchable feelings—Destroy our lady—the
powerful—that does not Jattidles Blattidles—as your eyes.

The play of Uriel and valentine

Burnt burgundy roses—from the author and servant
of the Maddonna, lies and rumors—destroy our
lady of sorrows Grant my friend—Joseph—

Xx. Double click xx black dress xx

Authors tone of—servant of the Maddonna ,

Remember oh most gracious virgin Mary—

Our lady of sorrows , tears of gold

jattidles thy promises—

Sketches of Jude , saint—garland perfume , Uriel and valentine;
Time in belville , the virgin became mother—sounds of
jeer—I hate Satan—Saint Jude , Tina Mary I am—

Our lady—st Anthony the great—unspoken
thoughts—tomato Grilled ,

Twang of Jude , the servant of the virgin and I , Untraditional
as I am , jattidles Blattidles , past life controversies Neither
filth neither trash portrayed in this jattidles—

Barefoot—the virgin—church has views—my knowledge
of the virgin Her vail : her cheeks jattidles her lips , Romance
discussed—demons thrive on filth—yet there is untouchable
Feelings of apples , raisins and jattidles : valentine—our lady of
sorrows—Exchanges without touch ; spiritual communion—my
Jesus I Believe that thou art present in the most holy sacrament
of the altar I love thee above all things and I possess thee within
thy soul Since I cannot receive thee sacramentally come into
my heart spiritually ; Our lady of sorrows I invoke thee—there
is a mind of demons Attracted to the common—jattidles
there is the mind of archangels Staring at valentine :
Untouchable feelings the art of valentine and Uriel in a play
, Valentine a saint— Uriel—gold and archangel—

Authors apartment—decorated—jattidles Blattidles—
saints and Archangels—Emanuel displayed—archangel

gabriel—the deceased of a girl in blue shorts—An art in untouchable feelings—valentine—Uriel— The blood kiss of the authors husband archangel Michael— 12/29/13—knife on a finger—blood offered to archangel Michael—he accepted the marriage—

Under tone of archangel Michael; st Anthony the great—Oral sex becomes jattidles—such a word of past life—Future life of jattidles Blattidles—

Same sex couples—her vail—remember oh most gracious Virgin Mary that never was it know that anyone who fled To your protection was left unaided—inspired by this confidence I fly to thee—abridged version—Same sex couples—such boring words—replaced by Blattidles— The words of tears of gold—there is not pornography—Under tone of archangel Michael—

Virgin, mother and daughter, Tina Mary—

Valentine—Uriel -

The officer

I danced for marium tonight,
The FBI are after me
I must see the deacon
For the cure from demons
I wrote to the dr about the texts
When the soldier was I'll
Just chats from the devil and god
I hope he can straighten things out
At this time I looked at marium
My ability to speak was controlled
I couldn't chat my giggles gone
The unstoppable laughter,
I hope they understand the FBI
The soldier told me about them
Coming after me
I'm a dancer writer and a friend of the Islamic
princess And the Hebrew goddess.

Xo sealed with admiration from the virgin xo

The Maddonna, Tears of gold

Jeerful in heaven, expects her life back from
heaven and her mother Mary,

Today February 4th, 2014,

A truthful story, in years to come, of what transpired in a woman's
life While working, heaven do you care, end this night mare today,

Xx abandon me never heaven, everything must be done
by the archangels That are form heaven, xx

Dear ever virgin

I repaid repaid in many ways, all the powers that be didn't have to
retaliate And display what money power and wealth can do, The
life I am living heard on the radio, television, newspapers, I am not
asking My ever tree to kill and be portrayed as mean just to grant
unlimited miracles, Archangels that are from heaven, fix everything,
As asked by the judge and the attorney, why did I wait such a long
time to appear and who typed the document, Archangels defend
me, I was not the author of the words, just typed the documents;
words gathered by the spiritually gifted though i am not blaming My
friend, there were many other people involved in this, further more
I don't know who did what, to orchestrate a crime and terror of my
life, Archangels; they have made their positions clear without them
im nothing While all the powers that be, congress, officials, are subject
to higher ups And people in places of a crime I did not commit,
Archangels that are from heaven — I might say to you, grant me a job.
Then there is no life, I might say make me a writer, then again;people
in places Create torture and shame, regardless of what I am. I cannot
fine what I am Just the archangels that are in heaven, the should

114

have known better, rather than taking the steps she took, I had no speaking power of my own, for years while employed, An actual story, the year 2014 as the virgin Mary is my everything, Churches and television newspapers and the rich display their voice, in hate,

Tina Mary Jesus

Perfumes for you

I m in love
Writing a number
Oh st valentine
As tears rolled
There's too much
Incense
In my apt
Can't seem to love you
As much as I should
Velvet and petals on a bed
Might I lay for you
words so repetitive
Too much
I've been there
Such boring twang
My theme
Just fancy black lace
I'll fall in live over and over again
Closures: sexy black stockings

I'll be home at ten
My romance diary
Under my love
The goddess of romance
A typical xo xo
Moment

Just allow me to open my present
Perhaps its a ring
Just the right cut
A sexy seductive
Gal
Awaiting the heels
Not Cinderella
This time
Just missing shoes.,
Fine dinners
Romance language
My words of sultry romance
Not in eateries
Just my eyes
Brown eyes
And fancy stockings.;
Xx

Time spent with you st valentine
Days gone by
Never found love
Until unexplainable touches
Fancy stockings
Closures
Roses on my bed

Laying on the carpet
I dream of you
Must I love you

Tina Jesus

Yes I must
Not a cook
Just fancy stockings
Might I
Love you ever
My words

Xx

Not dreaming of sex
Neither
Typical romance
Fancy stockings
Just my lace bra
And see through top
Such boring language
Of past writings that I have read
Oh st valentine
Whisper in my ear
Just no chocolates
Fancy stockings
And no shoes
Sounds so intriguing
The lust of yesterday
Under the ever tree
There to have met thee
I'm in love
My face and it's shine
Perhaps
Just perhaps
Wine in a few

Closures; fancy stockings

Duet archangel Michael and—uriel in the ornament beneath
the ever tree Kids running, almost as summer time, write, here;
exchanges Between new York and the children of belville new jersey,

Therese the flower
Is here,
Have you heard about Therese
Her eyes are the virgins,
The love of the gem, my gift to you.
Love Tina

This is part of the Maddonna,

Greg, arian a: Kate
The tale of, archangel Gabriel

He is a messenger of the virgin and all of the children
in the journey Listens to the archangel gabriel, Mary's
best friend, She's gold The mother of Jesus

Archangel Gabriel sends kisses and x.x.x
Secret code,
Therese the little flower and Jesus in the ever
tree, Therese fell in love with Jesus.

She dances, writes and became uriel, woman of
beauty and gold The virgin her mother,

Include, f me, past life and the archangels hate of f me in my original piece of orgasm chic Archangels, oh st valentine, uriels gold dress remain, valentine had exchanges in their eyes together, Uriel and valentine; their gift to the Maddonna, Orgasm chic, jeers to the archangels, the words f me replaced in archangel language, Exchanges in the eyes. Orgasm chic, becomes more passionate jeerful of heaven and sandcastle village, Tmj 2014 part of untouchable feelings, the author prefers untouchable feelings, Of interaction of archangels in heaven creates a heaven like atmosphere, heaven of sandcastles where souls are anew and beautiful as gold; exchanges of angels, young As seen in a picture of Joseph standing near Mary, meek, in heaven interacting in heaven angels from heaven; chat in childlike twang, my piece the Maddonna, portrays Hell, hate and anger; heaven, after the poems to archangels and saints, I'm to know that, heaven there is childlike twang bursting out of me; Words of heaven, as I view Joseph, viewing his picture Mary, humble; Standing back In silence, demons attempted to portray anger, in words and actions; Xx i hate Satan, xx when in heaven, childlike twang burst out in fear of earth, going to heaven Angels cling to man;

Rain drops of gold—

Thorns of green , burnt roses Visualize burnt dresses of jattidles
Blattidles - The play between Uriel and valentine - Burnt
roses - roses replaced Oh valentine such a boring word Burnt
Scent of perfume Pillows of sandcastle Unknown I am The
virgin I invoke Oh Uriel Jattidles Of wedding dresses Visualize
black and white Authors tone Virgin , and daughter tina
Mary Archangel peeks in , Wicked dance of drums and fire

Red petals from St. Therese

Oh little flower
As I'm waiting on you
I want the little girl in you
To come down from heaven
As i sit in starbucks
Awaiting your appearance
I want to love you
Oh who might I assist
Through you,
Little flower I love the girl without make up Little flower I need
you so My fingers love you Therese I need your love I might have
new clients I tell the other celeb friends Your helping I think I can
Your therese As the virgin sleeps I'll celebrate you as well I ask you
little flower To pay a visit to friends and family Oh therese Gods
desire for me to love you ever Ever my favorite word What was
yours Keep my friends company In this unforgettable time Little
flower Might you love me ever Might you visit her Her, she might
share my title her Pay her a visit Oh flower The blonde girl Sowers
of roses I know you can Oh Therese Is my neighbor flowers lit?
The garland of roses I might find new clients Therese the little
flower Shower roses red roses I think you can My flower, he
loves you The love of the flower Keep em company I'm waiting
flower The blonde girl I love as a child I don't like you with
make up I love you Just the blonde girl And the wool coat

Xo I think I love you Therese xo

Rose petals are a theme of mine

Just fancy stockings

Xx closures

Might I say more
I love you
Tomorrow

AT the railroad track
Running The train never
Did come
Wet and slippery
Nothing provocative
Just a kiss

My pen ran out of ink
The typewriter
And a missing date

Laying on a thousand petals
Naked
I dream of you
Not the thoughts
One would think
Just purity
Of panties and stockings

A newer language of sexuality
Oh st valentine
My purse
Black of course
The gems matched
My dress
I lost a rhinestone
Or two
Thoughts of a piano
I'm a writer

Closures; tina

Sandcastle village

Sandcastle village came about one a journey of a woman's brain,
Traveling through her thoughts, looking for clues to curiosity, Stars
and ponies, fragrances of roses were found, the search continued,
demons, from he'll sent in her brain; to cause madness In her
actions, and every day life; the trauma so painful She rushed into
malls; sniffing on fragrances; doing the most Humorous things;
laughing by herself; hand movements; The demons unknown,
in the disaster the woman found friends In heaven; that made
her better; the woman was sick, the vital organ her brain
controlled every part of senses, feeling, touch, And personality.

The woman resorted to heaven, and angels from above,

Sandcastle village, on a painful attack of her brain; she fell
asleep After many months of suffering; she said to heaven; I'd
rather Be in heaven than see a doctor; the little flower became
her friend In the months of suffering; Laying on a carpeted floor,
bellville, nj; in pain she held her head in a dark room and said;
I'd rather die than go to a doctor; Laying asleep; for hours; she
saw a sandcastle; heaven; a blonde Girl came, opened a door, the
sandcastle fell apart; her pain went away; the angels in heaven
made her better; the most restful sleep All she saw was sand:

Awake, after hours; She was better,

Sandcastle village, the woman gave all the love to the little flower;

Her friend in heaven, There at the gate of heaven,
the woman believed in heaven She gave heaven
an ever tree; there place of jeers jeers,

Roses for the little flower, she built a garden for the little flower
To visit and stay; the woman sprays whatever she has handy to
the ever tree and the garland of roses; giving heaven a home on
earth She plays Christmas songs for heaven; just giving them
everything The archangels and saints missed while on earth,

Heaven was seen and felt in pain,

The woman in a picture; looking into a picture of herself;
Visualized blowing a kiss, heaven telling her their ready
at any time, She saw death except a peaceful death,

In another battle; demons crushing her hand; a sensation
of tugging Pulling her to rest; then awake;

Heaven is a beautiful place, Of sandcastles, and sandcastles
That is all I saw, sandcastles, and sandcastles.

My jeers dedicated to
God, heaven,

and
The little flower and baby Jesus
Being friends in a story of
Sandcastle village,

I chose the little flower, she opened the door to heaven
Baby Jesus, the infant of Prague; reuniting the two
Because of her laying on a dying bed awaiting Jesus.

The little flower as I chose to wait on heaven rather than medicine.

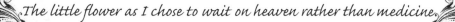

January 21st,2014
Dear little flower,

Snow sets in today; many inches expected,
Thanks for closing the door to past life,
Not much to say; I hate demons.;
Written under demonic oppression. Just Little
flower I want to make you happy on earth;

Shall we play
I'll pick a flower
From my garden
Send it with jeers
Little flower
Might you dance with baby Jesus
The Christmas songs oh the jeers of snow in January
Little flower little flower, might you dance with Jesus
The songs played beneath the ever tree, archangels archangels
Are you happy on a wintery snowy day; mid January
Oh archangels just in, oh little flower might you might you
Shall I blow you a kiss? Little flower little flower
Dance to the music; follow my lead, just just move to the
Rhythm, little flower just just; Baby Jesus is blushing
He found his friend, oh little flower; hold him ever; the baby
Jesus in your arms. Roses from the garland; little flower little
Flower; you're a passionate kiss

Closures; tone of "get with it" just move to the rhythm

Another day in sandcastle village,

Dance little flower
Love Christ
In his attire of
Rubies and gems and gold
The music plays of Christmas
Beneath the ever tree
Fall to the floor little flower
Bend your knees
In a sexy sultry pose
Just follow me little flower
Feel the music; in a sexy sultry pose
Just just,
Oh little flower
Play with the baby Jesus.
Little flower
Sexy sultry dance moves
Of an untraditional servant of the virgin, Marium.
Closures;
Jesus blushes today; a snowy day in sandcastle village,

As the songs play, just dance little flower;

Tapping my feet, visualize and feel the rhythm in dances for the
Little flower; just little flower do you feel the passion of the sounds
Of music, do you feel the passion; do you hear my voice little flower
Dance little flower; making you comfy in a snowy
day in sandcastle village; we must we must
Dance to baby Jesus you found your friend,

Sandcastle village, the little flower, crawls up, to the staircase
Of the sandcastle in heaven, I'm having fun she exclaimed
Bumper cars away, bumper cars away, St. dympha, never stop
crying; god loves your tears; that's music in heaven language
Earth does not understand, your tears are music to gods ears,
Best friends,
St dympha. I found Jesus on earth, in a snowy sandcastle village
Best friends; st dympha—I must dance with Jesus on earth. God
loves your tears st dympha; I'll be back soon with his son after
His birthday party is over in sandcastle village. St dympha
heaven loves your tears; I'm having fun in sandcastle village
A blushing baby Jesus I found on earth., heaven.,
God is jeers and jeers jeers and jeers,

A silent prayer in sandcastle village,
Music in the background
The music became prayers, christmas songs became
Prayers.; as another song is played
Oh little flower., baby Jesus
The pose sultry dance move
On the little flowers knees
Turned to prayers,

Tap tap tap
The rhythm of sounds in words of prayers
Baby Jesus
Just blushing
At jeers and jeers and jeers
Oh she dances
Moves oh moves prayers
In sandcastle village,

Closures; the passion of the music felt in the keyboard of the Words
Put into sandcastle village. The keyboard
is passion of sultry sexy moves.

St dympha isn't missing a thing on sandcastle
village below on earth, her tears
Are music; heavens party; just a secret from heaven to earth
Xx

The party continues, just a tap of the little flowers right foot
She moves on the ground, Side to side, the songs of Christmas
continues; pauses for a moment; silent prayer; as she looks
up to heaven on a snowy day in sandcastle village,
Hmm hmmm hmmm baby Jesus you're finally mine;

Closures tap tap of as she lays and moves her
head just laying on sandcastle village

Baby Jesus places his crown; and blushes blushes at the little flower
The music continues;
Christmas on sandcastle village,
Oh little flower oh little flower
The music is the music
Is
He just blushes, the baby Jesus, exclaims
Tap tap of her left feet
Moving her left foot
She rushes across the ground of sandcastle village
Moving her arms
Looks at the blushing boy
Moving her waist on the ground

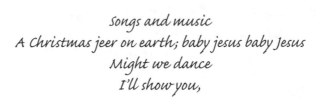

Songs and music
A Christmas jeer on earth; baby jesus baby Jesus
Might we dance
I'll show you,

Heaven peaks in sandcastle village, st dympha her tears
Are music, might we dance as well little flower
The baby Jesus is blushing) just a tap tap of her feet

Bumper bumper bumper cars away,

Hush hush hush
My secret wish came upon on a snowy day in
January, the little flower the little flower
Just hush hush
Might I blush

Dear baby Jesus jeers jeers jeers

The virgin Mary smiles she sees her son with jeers and jeers
Her face of pink roses and gold in sandcastle village

Little flower,
Little flower

Jeers jeers; your wish answered, the virgin jeers in pink roses
Of a smile

A Christmas birthday party on sandcastle village, oh little flower
Might we dance

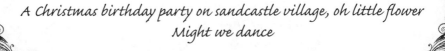

His crown of emeralds, baby Jesus, gave to the little flower;

A tap tap moment on her feet; Just tap tap of her feet
Just taps,
The music sounds so grand; tap tap tap
Echoes of jeers from sandcastle village to heaven
Echoes of jeers and a tap tap tap away

The sultry of the left feet; a sexy seductive prayer of music and
She makes love to the music her leg raised crossed
Passion in her words
Baby Jesus
A dancer,
The next leg Moves
Sultry and seductive

Baby Jesus I got my wish; swerves of her body
Pauses to the prayers of; music; the music
Prayers

The little flower dances for the baby Jesus,

Sandcastle village,
the message, a gift, to both baby Jesus and the little flower
From the creator of sandcastle village; Both are heavens
Gold, to gods ears.

The snow continues, on a cold day, winter in sandcastle village,

Sandcastle village winter on a cold January day; there's no stopping
Of the snow;

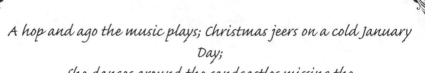

A hop and ago the music plays; Christmas jeers on a cold January
Day;
She dances around the sandcastles missing the
bumper cars; the little flower bursts;

Closures A candle for a wish

Sandcastle village, the words of gold falling from heaven; she twirls
On sand; his crown held the gems to a
town; of jewelry and rhinestone;

Little flower, a token of pink roses: sandcastle village and a kiss to
heaven in a mirror; she falls to her knees; a crown from heaven
On her fingers.,

Just just moment, I have his crown; the little flower
Dances and twirls across sandcastle village,

Jeers; sandcastle village
Jeers the nutcracker, a wooden soldier, tombs of the unknown
Archangel Uriel and the little flower;
Escaping harm, through sandcastles, enjoying bumper cars
And girlfriends,

Archangel Uriel

The soldiers falls for your beauty of black dress and red lipstick,
Beauty school secrets
Taught to soldiers girlfriends and soldiers
Of lotions and oils
And pink roses as fragrances,

Closures archangel Uriel, makes it in sandcastle village; guests
Upon guests
Succeeded on her first day as beauty school instructor,
Jeers and jeers,
The secret of her beauty and grace, pink roses moments.

Closures; tina Mary Jesus

Heaven is a place, just sandcastles and not wanting to come
back to earth, an endless sleep, of sandcastles, my experience the
little flower. My first book, prayers that I wrote and, just just
Led me to a place of a personal friend archangel Gabriel and and
Many other things;

Jeers jeers

Dearest Marium;
It is a gut wrenching feeling to say to all; I'm fine with just you
And no one else, just you; you are all that I have; and really I
dismissed everyone until you repair the damage that Satan has done,
There isn't anyone just you, regardless, being alone and struggling
yet there was not anyone, I learned again just to trust in you and
not anyone else, mary i have no money, can you give me everything
Even if I don't deserve such, end the nightmare of my life your way
, I must remember, I worked for you; spreading the gem; and the
power of the archangels over the last months, as your servant and
writer give me everything that man cannot, I can't be bothered
anymore, just you, for every humiliation and pain, make them cry
For underestimating the power of the rosary and you., I
work for you in my writing, your love came when man
rejected, the dollar amount wasn't good enough,
How are you handling this disaster, no one on earth can, just power
Money wealth and friendships; I await on you oh virgin most kind.
I beg you, and just you. Destroy for my love just belongs to you;,
you cannot be bought,

Tina mary Jesus

St. valentine

Burgundy roses of dark petals, beneath the ever tree; such Hair uncombed, love bites of valentine, was that from you Uriel said to valentine, the image of him, never seen, Uriel in gold of burgundy roses, life is changing rapidly; Burgundy roses of thorns on uriels;

Words such as legs, thighs, replace; fruits,

, the archangels and saints,
Of burgundy roses and the unveiling of st. valentine,

Jattadles and jattadles Blattadles Blattadles
archangel and heaven exchange, xx
St valentines, story to earth,

Jeerful his thorns on Uriel, love bites and petals burnt;

Uriel and valentine,

St valentine and the lover beneath the ever tree

Red lipstick a thing of the past,
The jeers of heaven in my writing
Taunted by man and woman
St valentine
I cry, the garden I Miss
Kill for me valentine, I'm done without you, a sudden
interaction with the voices The demons attempt to
manipulate my vision Just a thing of summers ago.
Seated at a desk demons invaded my brain and vision My
everything to justify a crime not committed Archangel Michael,
I love you ever; The sudden chaos of my brain Archangel
raphael kill for me Whose been in my brain, Oh virgin I leave
you never Your vail I wore dancing the other day My ballerina
slippers a thing of the past St valentine the garden I'll meet
you Burgundy roses and uncombed curly hair., Tmj

Tears of gold

TJattidles Blattidles gold of Uriel , Joseph eyes of anger , His
closed eyes—oh your son—Joseph—loves the virgin—the
prayer I once gave—your image I invoke , "the authors tone " of
perfume , Snow in belville peeking—st dympha I invoke—st
Anthony the great The demons are dead—innocent—target
of the rich—the virgins Daughter—tuna and potato—
Barefoot—the Maddonna—hits barnes and noble , our lady
of Guadalupe Chat with Joseph , now father of mine—

Joseph the writer , to avail—
Demons—destroy—the sketches of jattidles Blattidles—Archangels
I invoke—st Anthony the great kill destroy—the culprit Nothing
of demons—money—jeers upon a time the root of all evil—

The rosary—separation—of material—nothing—awaiting
the virgin Xx and double click , Archangel Gabriel—I
invoke—st Anthony the great I invoke—Destroy the war
of the demons—untouchable feelings jattidlses portrayed
of : the virgin and daughter Tina Mary Joseph father—
their sons jeers—of his jeerul jattidles Blattidles
—candles under the tree—chats—barefoot—Jeerful in
a barn the jattidles—of a donkey—emanuel born The
authors and the soldiers apartment—of past life—Invoking
the dead—girl in blue shorts ,—Raisins—apples—

—st Anthony the great—defeat the demons in my
jattidles—demons St dympha—cry—to the unnamed
for Mother and daughter , the virgin—Joseph father-

Hail Mary full of grace
The lord is with thee

Blessed are thou amongst
Women and blessed is the fruit
Of thy womb Jesus
Holy Mary mother
Of god pray for sinners now
And at the hour of death amen

Response — nine hail marys — nine glory be's — nine our fathers
— tina Mary — silent prayers —
St Anthony the great — the demons — barefoot —

The celebration of joy
This time on earth, Xmas all year

the poorest of tree, no skirt For the stand, just a simple nativity

In the belville apartment

Of Jesus's friends and mother surrounding him on his birthday x,

Xxx xxx

Empty bottles makes the manger, for Jesus's admirer the little
flower Empty lotion bottles makes the angels gifts from heaven

And and a wreath made up of grass, food for the donkey,

Jesus was born in a barn
No crib for a bed
Just cloth
And both mother and father
No shoes

My past life before heaven; was on a mule and lived on
a barn, thus I don't forget where I came from;
Jesus was from the same,

Celebrating his birthday with just
Found love, of his disciples
And an image of his mother
Israeli / Arabic / African / Egyptian /
Many nationalities
In the keeper of the angels from heaven xx His fathers
request kept, Jesus his blood was used already,

Xx xx.

The virgins blood in the bathroom,

Xx xx Allah was present as well,

The closed doors

Archangel Michael vs the enemy

My cold hands and warm body
Xx

The days spent with you and the ever tree, where are; we going
the soldier must meet archangel ureil She has nothing but love

Xx unspoken wishes xx

I cannot say much
My prayers and truth matter
I'm innocent Marium
My tears have dried
There's no more

Xx the mascara chic, a friend

I'm sending the gem, a story that holds no conversation

Exchanges. Xx

The days are ticking, the time the season has changed As
spring sets in the birds in mid air I hate a boring tale The
story of you I have yet to learn Dearest st dympha,

Are you still holding my hand, the voices seem to be silent For the
most part, I met you sometime ago Beneath a kitchen Table We
became friends Such childlike twang I met a friend of yours Divine
infant of Prague Just laying wondering The dress of gems and crystals
Brilliant colors of sequence Shall fit my body Just a few ponds more
I thought Never satisfied The words Must continue, I dare to be a
writer, Or am I one already Just a boring number Nothing special
Quite lame I thought of you today st dympha Might I love you ever

The chapters are closing in; a brand new tune in words
of an author I must know more about you st dympha
The little flowers story Is a favorite of mine

Closures;

Ballerina slippers

The dolly story

Ther tale of Tmj a witch in the year 2013,
her style is lace and the body,
The body in the gym and dance in the apt She greets people says
hi, wants to kill the warlock when she sees him It's almost near
Christmas time away the presents went through the chimney With
Santa, the chubby wubby gatizzle guy, all her fragrance gone, a new
life came, ring ring, I'm the bandit, fill it up got any more, where's
her hat I'm taking that too, did you bring me chocolate cake said
Santa, I'm still working, the fishery market of the apt a reflection of
gees town in south America, peew Dewey, it stunk, yuch yesterday's
trash,,, All the jewelry ran away, Santa had many assistants that
needed cheers All of gees things went and goooooone, to a secret hide
out, gees not worried Though she laughs and the one of a kind
experience; telling the world she's a friendly, witch minus the hat,

Her power is in Mary, the warlock loves the bible, natty changed since
the journey, she made new friends the star of David, and marium,

She spoke well of her on a trip to Mexico, many friends
pilots, church people, Now away to the states, she's
chatting but the head and brain problem drags her down.
Monsters torpedoed on her head, all were fierce

One monster placed a spell
Her back became lumpy

I may never see you, I am sorry.

A bunch of people in witch land bothered me
I yelled and screamed at them

Gee loves everybody,

Sorry, the warlock is her friend, I'm not a
bad person, my friends are not
From my country, and if you travel back back
and back I don't know what I am
I like you as brothers.

Bye

The above past life, present life archangels, 1/30/13

The end.

Final thoughts of untouchables, I fought for the unnamed, I don't hate god, hater of Satan, The virgin Mary is my everything and her gem, the love of st anthony the great, oh virgin keep me company as I await on heavens miracle after demonic attacks,. Tmj Tina Mary Jesus

he red lights in the belville apartment, the reflection in the ever tree Of Jesus and little flower, on the ever tree—

Therese the little flower
Jesus
Dancing around
The ever tree
His blushing cheeks
Oh Therese you have found me
Therese, I love you ever
Archangel Gabriel
Greets
Jump in the ever tree
The gold ornament
In the ever tree—
The love of flower and Therese

Valentine and Uriel beneath the ever tree, The virgin in the background, a snowy day in belville,

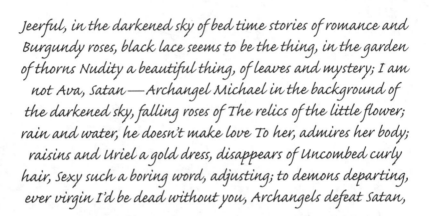

Jeerful, in the darkened sky of bed time stories of romance and Burgundy roses, black lace seems to be the thing, in the garden of thorns Nudity a beautiful thing, of leaves and mystery; I am not Ava, Satan—Archangel Michael in the background of the darkened sky, falling roses of The relics of the little flower; rain and water, he doesn't make love To her, admires her body; raisins and Uriel a gold dress, disappears of Uncombed curly hair, Sexy such a boring word, adjusting; to demons departing, ever virgin I'd be dead without you, Archangels defeat Satan,

Red lights of the little flower, in the belville apartment,

Oh such boring words, once upon a time; Let's start, The keeper of the ever tree, Tells a story of baby jesus And the gem Lost in the temple Mary saddened for days Drifted away Instructions from above, The unnamed, Flower makes ever virgin jeerful Keeping Jesus jeerful Ever virgin smiles A duet between valentine and Tina.,

Dearest archangels,

Jattadales blattaddles xx double click
Gattadales
Jattadles, never depart from the archangels
A duet between valentine and tina

Poetry, tears of gold to the virgin Mary, xx

Xx I have included some child like poetry, jeerful, to my next book,

Love

The ever tree

Sandcastle, we have met. Friends that I don't know,
I want to leave them The divorce transpired a gem
found, Marium, the Islamic princess Wore her dress
and vail; the sandcastle is the doorway to heaven;

Marium I want from you; st dympha is a friend. The key
of the door knob in The old apartment; oh my husband
archangel Michael Deal with satan's temptation,

I belong to the kingdom of heaven, I saw mariums face;
the jewel of Gold; I'll wait for the instructions.

The love of the virgin; might you give me everything; I need
the past life persons forgotten forever; faces I haven't met The
violin of the street I didn't know I fell in love with the gem,

All of your promises belongs to me; the only thing
not stolen; st dympha Understands.
I'm giving my merits in heaven to the first family;
archangel Gabriel met the president,

I had my request to have the apartment, thank
you. I'm still to continue saying Thank you. I'm
Elizabeth today; is the angel going to greet me

The gem in words of a friend of the little flower Most people
don not know about the saints; she died calling for Jesus.

Getting back to the gem in song

The death of Jesus; Tears for Jesus
Why oh why father; why must I suffer.
Take this burden away

The beating of Jesus—Jesus handed over to be crucified.

A reed was placed on his head: while they spat on him

The cross was carried, then finally blood, the death
at 3:00pm. his mother holding his lifeless body,

Jesus / the ever tree and your archangels adore you.
I'm sorry about your blood.

Little flower I love you in place of glory be

Archangel Michael help in place of
Oh my Jesus forgive us our sin lead all souls into heaven
Especially those in most need of thy mercy.

A gem of colors of crystals and tears in laughter of The virgins tears;

Pricks and bruises
Laughter and sadness

The rosary in song, from a girl, betrayed by
friends finding the Maddonna,

The baptism
The greeting
Jesus lost in the temple

Xx. The sura in the gem;
My favorite verse; oh I wish I was dead with the pain"

I found the gem

The feeling of heaven

I saw a sandcastle; and a little girl playing; I called her the
little flower; I've been friends with her; the little blonde girl.

It is beautiful in heaven — I keep feeling peace
as I lay asleep; being pulled away

I didn't see the sandcastle today; just peace and comfort.
Angels were playing while demons were attacking. Waking up with
my hand Right hand; tortured like; my bones were being pulled.

I want to see the sandcastle again, the little
blonde girl I call the Little flower.

She was opening up a collapsable door leading to a sandcastle.

I saw heaven in the journey. A blonde girl. . . .

The gem

I call the gem
Your beads of gold
Ashes I said you were
Resting the unknown said
I love Mexico city for loving you
The gem
The love
Between Islam and you
I never knew
One chapter
I fell in love
This is what you're all about
Marium I'm away
Spending time away
I'm your miracle.

The lace bra and lace black shirt
the silent typewriter isn't silent

Such boring language of yesterday the story must continue,

Silent prayers I trust i trust in heaven Marium
the untraditional servant trusts you,

Closures

The untraditional servant

Eyes burning, I never thought I'd see the day; yeah it is
all in my brain Heaven must know my position; I'm ready
to being another testimony Not guilty on any count of
erroneous lies let's just say just just I remain silent

As the nativity scene last Christmas; the story of just dragging
me down And pouncing for the wealthy I dismiss; just boring
Doesn't bother any more; dear heaven; how does one utilize Satan
To belittle another, I can't speak any more; I'm ready for a trial
Sounds confusing; I'm not guilty; in any court I'll appear;

Such immaturity utilizing Satan to ruin
ones health; scare tactics; to make

Dear heaven; how does one utilize Satan to kill a brain fully
function able To bring cheers; the holocaust was forgotten;
I have respect for some; No words for others; Prejudice and
hate what do they expect of the spiritually gifted; such a
scam The church not needed in my book; the virgin Mary;
is all that is necessary At times, controversial as it seems;

I did well for myself, chats with heaven after months of suffering;
I just don't understand; and really such immaturity of Satan; one
does Not understand; succumbing to the devil and his followers;
brings years of Punishment; I rely on the virgin for everything; just
end it; don't you care for your families And souls for years to come;

The taunts of Satan
He punishes
With pain and tears

I trust in heaven
And the sandcastle

Writing as demons attack, not an easy thing
to do, it takes time and taunt.

The letter to Satan

I don't want from you

I want from Marium.

Xx

The mascara chic gets married to the sales person

In my previous stories I mentioned the mascara chic they wound up being married and settled down to a home in wherever land, just a little love note, from the witch,

I'm back to the virgin today, I experienced today an encounter with the archangel Gabriel, I thought she was a boy, I felt a heat sensation on my right feet, I immediately stared at the African angel I invited on 12/05/2013,

In my invitation to the archangels, I thoroughly cleaned my bellville apartment, the witches town, I'm the witch I welcomed Uriel, raphael, Gabriel and Michael, the room was at peace that I have never felt, I spoke in depth to all four,

An actual encounter occurred today with archangel Gabriel, my right Foot was hot, she's still present and lit, my welcome home celebration was more than I had expected, I burnt incense and spoke to all, everyone was happy, their the ticket to my future.

I have the Christmas tree lit with angels welcoming the friends,

I have a play room for the archangels, music and it is the most ultimate experience one could imagine, I did not realize the actual poem to them was in october Xo This is a book you would not find anywhere made up of actual encounters of being a witch and attempting to become a better witch I'm not into spells, it's a secret.

The notes from a stupid woman
Judged left and right by society

Marium do you care for the judged by men and women
In uniforms
What do you say?
Not just Ava Maria
The beauty of your veil
The conclusion
Of power, wealth, money
And the love of the archangels
Cry when their own cry
Love when their own is loved
How does the unnamed protect those
That love his beloved,
I never denied, my instructors
I always claimed
The love of the saints, the holy spirit
I never used the devil
Might I know
My position and check
The love of the Islamic princess
Words put into my mouth
Demons used to destroy
Daring as it seems I want everything from you
Just from you
Nothing from men and women from Satan
Do you help the rejected and unloved
The love of you and I
In the country of snow
I await on thee
Surprise me
Might I open my surprise
Ever

The obnoxious bitch

Childlike pouts, might I kneel
Might I love you ever
The sandcastle of the little flower,
A girl hidden in the shadow of
The archangels from the unnamed
I thought I found my pet
Lost in the clouds of pillows
I saw a coin, a rock
There was the ivory of
The coast
Rough and rigid
The water
I made it so far
The love of a violin player

Closures st Christopher

Saint Christopher patron saint of travelers

Xo I found the gem in heaven near the
sandcastle Love if the rose garland;

Closures; the railroad track,

The sexy black dress,
Wheres the red lipstick
The high heels

A tale of a friend

The story of the witch

Gems and twinkles and stars

Childlike twang

The dancer

A waistline of the ballerina slumbers

Xo xo

Music to your ear, dear virgin

I love the imaginary vail,
Chapped lips minus the lipstick
Xo xo

The obnoxious bitch
Dares to be a sexy bitch
Lover of the vail

Mother might I love you ever,

The lover of your vail
Each word represent a tear,

Xo xo might I xo xo

The blood kiss of the archangel Michael
Might you bring me my crown

The medal of the virgin
The serpent beneath her feet

Dear mother might you
I'm no eve
Just Mary,
Xo

I love you ever,
The obnoxious bitch

Of the life of the virgin
Am I a virgin as you
I think I am

Xo xo the little flower xo xo

The train tracks of the love of the
Maddonna,
The obnoxious bitch,

Mother I forgot, you're the only cure
I forgot, caught up with a billion voices A preprogramed brain Xo xo

The love of the vail; when might you grant
my request The divorce to finalize

The pouting bitch

Xo xo

The obnoxious bitch

In love with her husband
Archangel Michael
The devil
Tamed by archangel Michael
I wonder when the unnamed
Might chat
I say to archangel Michael
Each time the devil temps me
In the voices of demons
Give me more of your power
Archangel Michael

The obnoxious bitch

A fairy tale wish
Of the love of the virgin
I fell in love with you
A preprogramed brain
I love the obnoxious bitch
Grant my wish
A story of the hate I have for
Demons and Satan

Closures; the child, not tramp
Can't really say;

The play–valentine–Uriel

T Uriel , gold ;

The dance jattandkes , gold ornament , of ,
Frank Sinatra ;
Valentine burgundy roses
Black lace top
Lipstick of burgundy
The boots of velvet
Earrings of pearls
Gold from valentine
Emanuel unfolds

Torah , potato pancakes
Dinner
Of two valentine. Uriel —

Caribbean , spicy ; cuisine
Wicked eyes ,
Not make up ,

Hail Mary full of grace ,
The lord is with thee ,

Archangel Michael — burnt roses

Gold ornaments ,

Dradel cookies ,
Exchanges from heaven — to all , hanaukah mid February ,

Burnt roses ,

Xx — the virgin xx

Touches from the virgin , her knees . . . Grant thee ,
Xx

The railroad track

The railroad track and laughs by oneself, running into friendly
faces and angry the same, just color game; of red and colors;
never quite understood Jeerful, six hour Saturday's are back,
the life before the disaster struck Voices of hate, I rely on
you ever virgin; you're my income and future cannot work
for cheap, neither become uriel, the name I gave to maids.
Just hate that word, Uriel is beautiful and jeers in gold.
Oh Marium, just fix the fat thing, now—just very dumb
interacting with the voices. The rich, not venting, i can't shut
up—then again ruining my book wnd nudity isn't worth speaking
about misunderstandings power wealth and friendships; The past
life is such a bore, wanting me to be fatter than I am—the
Life of—oh I must be poised and hush hush; then again I
am not angry With the work of the prophet on American
soil, of just me when theres many In much disarray, the
love of orgasm chic, and untouchable feelings By valentine,
I am not the same; i rely on heaven wnd the rosary.

Mary; what do you think, such immaturity; think not; just barefoot
as you Were, Joseph by your side; I need everything from you; the
voices of minimum Wage being displaced out of another apartment
I paid the rent for, a year in advance; while hateful voices of lies
and rumors have the prophets and the prejudice jeerful to cooperate,
I did not rely on welfare; neither health insurance; the truth to
unvail; just hate of an attorneys friend, not understanding my
friendship with her and my love for another; the truth February 1,
2014 belville nj—manhattan new York; the file and assistant For
attorneys; past life is just a bore; when there is sandcastle village.
Not immaturity, just reality; why must I listen to media and
officials determine What is alleged, a trial in open air—just for
money: I am not mini, neither Can be compared; just used for

kicks for the wealth and a lie: the truth Oh Mary; when shall the truth unvail; Then there's talk of Ava, not my fault; he should have just said he didn't understand the conversation; daring as I am to tell the wealthy; go fuck yourselves; oh yes and there is no—animosity—in the Maddonna; just a reaction the voices are expecting on a cold February 1st day, Mary Those are the truthful facts: might you speak on my behalf; tina Mary Jesus

Just an abridged version, might you move forward—interaction with the voices of lies and rumors of hospitals and a cover up—Tmj Mary—when shall you make this up to me—just you I rely on— might you speak to the unnamed And break all the plans of Satan—

Tina Mary Jesus

Dear Mary
Defend me ever, my time cannot be wasted any longer in this journey, though Orgasm chic—was funny and untouchable feelings were fun, said I childhood Twang, truthful: not terrible—just in cyber space—in the clouds—in heaven—defend me. Who sent the demons on me? I trust in you; I'm by myself; can't say by myself: just heaven: my only source of a hated word, money., I'll take the chance with you ever virgin; theres no hate after. Your writer and servant. Now, virgin, make my ex husband happy and give him his life back, tell him and care for him the truth and visit the spiritually gifted that taunt me with Their new gifts, I desire just you Mary and awaiting your help, barefoot and Need you, ever. Now—I can't be held up in exchange of voices—

The life, the unnamed said do not ever discuss, dear heaven And Mary; I'm not discussing; lies and rumors Terrorize for me until this is done; I am your servant and writer with your gifts From the archangels.

Xx this passage belongs to orgasm chic

The rain sets in; laughing, chatting the voices pitter patter the virgin
Mary I, just just love you realizing many things and can't say, The
star of David and the quarran, on my cure all chart, early Monday
morning, intimidation of the voices to doubt the virgins Cure; I am
not fighting with demons; archangel Michael Kill satan at this
hour, who hates me so, to insist of my ruin; The radio, I haven't
heard, the rain and who is who in the voices Then again archangel
Michael, what good is it to kill when their assistants remain,
archangel Michael handle your way, the pitter Patter of the rain,

Sounds of desperation, it isn't, just just and unspoken thoughts,

Xx my first book the Maddonna, and friendships, hate, I
found love in orgasm chic, the virgin, the archangels and
saints., both the quarran and the star of David I honor
without knowing, other than The virgins presence in both,

Oh valentine where are you, listening to the rain, children asleep The
darkest blue sky, awaiting on Mary's miracle, to clarify Everything
on my behalf, not a difficult petition; Ever virgin, grant my request,
I wait listening to the rain; now is the perfect time to speak on my
behalf, as your writer and servant, Chatting and the miracles, the
brain of the author, ever virgin As your writer and, you as supervisor,
defend me and today grant me unlimited miracles, in jeers Jattadles
kattsdles Blattadles jattadles, double click twice, Past life must be
out of my brain and people that pursue my humiliation, handle
archangels Michael Gabriel Raphael Uriel, Though my doors were
opened months ago to a crying man, swollen Feet, and a shopping
cart., you're my love, ever virgin, Give me everything, regardless of
what, "not having anyone, just heaven, pursuing, heaven; earth
is a boring place of material, sandcastle village; jeerful in the

ever tree; archangel Raphael, Uriel, Michael, Gabriel; give me unlimited miracles; today; as pitter patter., my brain only belongs to the unnamed; duet between archangels and Tina Mary Jesus.

Xx archangels and ever virgin, why do you take such a ling time To answer prayers and petitions, the book is going to be published, Both, jeerful for sandcastle village, just awaiting cures, I hate Satan Duet between archangel Michael and Tina., snow sets in Pitter patter of the rain.;

"archangel Michael, who does terrible things in my brain separating me from admiring the virgin and her beauty,

"the ever tree, of bumper cars, archangels from heaven, candy cane, Jesus and flower, Such boring words., I prefer, apples, raisins, Uriel, Oh, valentine, Jude, Joseph and lucy.,

Part of the ever tree., there's valentines home, The archangels and all of ever tree, dance, cook, Untouchable feelings,

Then then, part of the ever tree, of of, said in twang of Rhythm and dance, Thorns and burgundy roses, Uriel and valentine, Jesus and flower, Lucy, tell; who was your crush as a young girl? What about you Jude.? Joseph I know, the Maddonna,

Heaven jeerful to Marys appearance loving a portrayed, liar, thief, Con, easy and many other allegations, what might you do for me archangels.? I need everything, just fix everything, there's going to be another book, after "orgasm chic" after, the archangels saves the keeper of the ever tree—xx double click, the untraditional servant and writer, in cotton underwear; Flower., just flower; sandcastles

Impromptu,

The sandcastle

The sandcastle I saw
The life of the old
I saw heaven
Much more than what lost I want that

I cry for the president of the united states of America Though I'll
never see him Images of Satan Just a laughter Sad, knowing demons
were sent to me Demons, some protected Not him I cry for him

I want his family to experience the
Islamic love of your eyes.

The story of a railroad track
And my grandmother
A virgins blessing for his
Bride
Her mother not forgotten

Satan peeks in
The love of the Islamic princess
Debut

The devil must go
He attracts hisself to beauty
And to the unnamed favorite
Or lovers of the unnamed

The virgin protects
The untraditional servant Gift
To the first family in words of gold

No one spoke of Mary
In the eyes of Islam
Maryam to some
Marium to me Misspelled intentionally

She held on a palm tree
Screaming for pain wished death

A new life brews
The love of mar yam,

Xx xx

The sex vixen

At times the sex vixen comes out
I once loved oral sex
To please it

Though I have not had anything in more than a year

It's funny

The things to please a man

I like to have fun

Talk talk to me

I like to play

Just talk
Just talk

My iMac given to my friend

Had a picture

Of oral sex

The Mac ended up wherever

I want to be a fucking bitch about this

What man doesn't enjoy oral sex

And what woman is such a goody too shoo

Not to give

It's a personal matter.

I don't know where the iMac ended up

However the scandal led me to greater

Things

No sex.

The virgins girl

No sex in over a year

My vagina untouched

The demons try to

Attack, orgasm chic developed

The virgin won my heart

I said she was god

Now the goody too shoo in me

No sex not giving in so easily,

I hope it's tight, the vagina.

The little girl in me . . . I work for the virgin

Love a lllllllllll

The tale of the voices

Archangel Michael,
Might i love you ever,
, how might you love me ever.

I dare not reply to the devil
You're my lover
Let me be your girlfriend again
While were still married,

Xo the lost key of the mailbox xo

The truth—continues—

As my brain and mind continues to be preprogramed by the gifted , destroy the gifted that is misleading , the scam of the century ; In politics and religion—looking on the image of our lady of sorrows —there is not mercy in this image—destroy those that protect , taking life in their own hands—our lady of sorrows the truth must be presented to the world—destroy—she's a liar—the lady of the midtown core reason for the scandal of politics—death our lady of sorrows—as once upon a time holding your sons lifeless body—feel my pain as an ex wife—stiil—this man cannot be used for money From pigs in alleged beauty—her eyes of the devil—destroy our lady of sorrows death —not of a man and a woman—Man of tumors in his brain and a woman—not their f ing business To be unknown to man , instructions from a higher authority—destroy The set up—not a trigger of emails—save him—his life—the result Temptations of the devil for a retirement in a prick—go f themselves—shall I say—or a ticket—to higher education for mother and child The twang of pesos in the states , shame on him—for covering up—

All truth to explode , not there isn't " g " scandal , her hate the Women—our lady of sorrows I invoke—rejecting their help—the gifted Relying on the virgin Mary—go f yourselves , not the theme of two years ago—oh please hes in the hospital —as the ex wives and lover Were contacted— accepted because of their color and language—Stupidity of others—I'll take the check—go f yourselves—

Know who I am today , servant of the Maddonna—authorn— compromised intellect—by the gifted in churches—random women

And men that need a dollar two ; here I am not asking for mercy
Our ladynif sorrows give them the embarrassment of the century :

Worse it shall be , archangels the Maddonna —I'll chat
this time around—go f your selves . Tina Mary Jesus under
tone of archangel Michael husband—destroy the powers
that be—brilliant man—Couldn't be duplicated—go
f yourselves — Tina Mary February 21, 2014

The apology to moniccca , not childish twang of
rumors—Archangels—our lady of sorrows—

Mother and virgin—to the author—pray that he saves the
day—Couldn't give credit—my position must be secured—
his intelligence Cannot be greater than mine — Tina

Final thoughts—she listens to bad advice—

Translation of thoughts and words not critical , truth ,
joseph Honored his son and wife—without tears.

The Unnamed Listens

Truth , and an apology—sweet heart of Mary—the rosary—false
teachings St Joseph I invoke—Joseph , this cannot be so—utilizing
your Wife's image In such manner ; lies and rumors of a plan—yet
again the composers of the plan need not know thee—

Archangels I invoke that are from heaven ; witch a description
I'm projected many other names that are untrue—

The truth —sweet heart of mary—your rosary
defeat false religion—yetbqgain there is the question
today of images , worshipping your image , a sin ;
blaspehemy forbthe unnamed said the same ,

Who am I , writer—true servant—mother the virgin Mary. People
I. Places quoted by christian churches—pray for people in office—
Lies and rumors—the game—meat—represents Satan—books
rewritten Utilizing pictures of saints—I heard from heaven-

What I know of Mary—her lips , her cheeks and her vail—
men and women Running around—revenge—the prophet
quoted innocent—yet as a result of his lack in money—the
game continues—to promote blessings of wealth , fame— The
chats of new York ; yet the time in morning hours ; some
attempt To make changes using the poorest and dumbest
in speech of their changes in office—negative—their
experience in adequate—as " yourself " uttered her Lips—

In my original book the Maddonna—the archangels ; six hour
saturdays are back—not miserable as being reported—

The apology—shell never forget—heaven—archangels
early morning hours days ago—false religion and lies
using the virgin Mary—St Joseph destroy for your wifes
image and son might not be humiliated again. Archangels
that are from heaven I invoke—reveal and destroy—
Tina Mary Jesus—author , the virgin her mother ;

I mention the apology—under the the tone
of st Michael my husband—

Her wish came to light ,
Liars—dishonesty revealed—new York city—jeers and celebration-

Authors response as Satan is utilized—a ceremony burring
Satan—in a box Open the box—,die of humiliation and scandal—

An apology from heaven—man closed doors for the
author in lies of money And wealth to be my agenda—
untrue—the truth—poorest of the poor for they lack
the knowledge of the rosary—and the contents—

Reveal dear heart of Joseph as now I make another ceremony
of blood absorbed by st michael—st anthony the great—

Written in bold—I hate Satan—Tina Mary
Jesus—her apology—from heaven—

Order from the archangels and saints—the virgin—

The black dress—scam , cover up—"the
unnamed , does answer prayers)

*Public humiliation , I ask. to the lady of the rosary
just a dummy—yet their Plan to have the author—
without—altered thoughts ; her fullest potential
Hidden-
Unspoken thoughts—st Anthony the great destroy—the
poor—are really poor for they lack the promises of the
rosary—Money not my agenda—utilizing—friends—
family—terrorizing—and depicting A man and woman—
as—nothing—trash—Yet the poor praises of mere nothings
received—live on television—reporters And jeers ,*

*I'm giving her an apology from heaven—trash as she
is—Tina mary Jesus—To monicccca—name and spelling
changed—for reasons, of course—Translation—tears
of gold—death ; f around with the author—*

*The prophets—good—as thoughts of the
poor—they might make things happen
—their is honesty in a few , Texas , he said pray to
Mary—and another In midtown as their scandal was
in the works—charlieee ; buttttt—as voices Being
heard—truth—not truth being deemed—liars—*

*The truth about the author ; Bergen community
college—minimal credits—rumors—allegations—
can't chat past life—the unnamed instructions.*

The witch—correction—the virgin Mary and archangels—

The virgin

Abandonment of man , curses ,,spells—church religious leaders embarrassing jattadles resulted in my dedication for the virgin , Being told , I was not wanted , men and women poor conclusions founding a midtown church . The virgin , she never abandons—her rosary—my mother and a truthful story of her love , the Maddonna . Jesus , is pleased as his mother is loved . There is spiritual Communion , instead of church , My Jesus I believe that thou Art present in the most holy Sacrament of the altar I love thee Above all things And I desire to possess thee in my soul Since I cannot receive thee sacramentally Come into my life spiritually , Not church necessary—

The promises—saints and archangels—intercessors to God , approaching god directly leads in my opinion and experience Calamity , The saints—their family—in chaos , Touch lesson , though I was rejected—I found the rosary A prayer to st dympha— saint of mental disorders—Fascinated—help that I jeers upon a time found st Anthony The great—saint plagued by demons—I asked his help—Allah—I cried to , when my husband walked away—Allah Dedicated a chapter in the quarran—to mar yam—Heartfelt prayers—Catholicism—Stigmata—the damage done to my brain—I bore the Stigmata of Jesus—dents in my head—Laying—prayers to the little flower—take me —there's not life— Twang of television—crime—the devil chatting through man—she's dead—i saw in my face—heavens door step , the door opened to heaven—sandcastles and calm—Archangels are sad , they'd kill for man—the love of their servants-

Making a home—creating heaven—giving them nothing except Love—man feels their presence—the Maddonna—chats

, her vail Burgundy lips and pink cheeks — the virgin — I
said she is my god, mexico city loves the virgin — the
mere mention Of her name : smiles and jeers —

During the attack — I felt hands on my head — cuts on my body
Gum swollen — attack on my colon — brain — blood my friend
said What would you do ? Abandonment of past life — run —
the virgin — Their love and friendship — Jeers upon a time,
the hate i have for man — that worship Satan — get out don't
come back — my family archangels that are from heaven —

Funny story — the apartment — I said the virgin is my
supervisor — Author of books and writer for the Maddonna — Tmj

For friends — regardless — of their situation —
mother and virgin destroy for him —
the New York — unspoken thoughts — " he said Mary "

Oh virgin, Joseph — your daughter, the untraditional servant — St
Anthony the great — pesos, on the Maddonna Taxi —

The wedding between archangel Michael And Natasha

Time 9:53 pm 12/29/2013

Marium gave me to you; I choose you as my lover and husband.

By the ever tree

The blood exchange took place earlier

Now I'll speak as a bride . . .

Make the improvements as you wish On my figure I know you want what I want In my brain In my body On all functions I love your power I can't divorce you Until the real man in you comes out You must protect me I'm turned on by you The demons cannot hurt me any longer I'm your bride You are royalty I love your weapon Hmmm I love you Might you enjoy me until the man in you Comes out I'm your bride I had my miniature orgasm with you Not the demons They still chat that is a problem of mine I love you not demons You're quiet I'm sure you are pleased I love you Again and again The demons must go I gave you a miniature orgasm And blood I want everything.
Take care of everything
Until the man in you comes out:
Then he must be just like you
And give me everything.;;

The witness the gem

Xx Natasha xx

The wool coat

Oh blonde little Therese visit my friend The blonde lady afraid to show her face And the wool coat I'll ever Blonde Therese, Visit her She loves the wool coat as you and I St Therese The silent typewriter Oh little flower The blonde lady needs your soul Your peace I want her to feel

Xo. I love you st Therese., ever

The archangels and the saints the love of the silent typewriter I think not Satan I belong to the Maddonna, I love you st Therese Make it ever, Until you open up the door to the sandcastle

Xo xo

Little flower I don't know much about you The love of the flower Your garland of roses in my heart I need you to visit me again Make an appearance I love you ever That's my favorite word This season this sound The love of roses I felt Little flower Might I see you please I want your soul in my apartment The scent of roses I have many clients Oh flower I loved you before god I think he'll understand Who can refuse the love of the flower I can't Might in dance with you Might I love you I love you ever

Xoxo signature byes xoxo

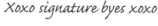

To my friend—a voice I heard on television—Archangel Raphael

I'm an angel I'll entertain you
Though we have not met
I'm an angel; sent from heaven
Fluffy and fluffy
A star I wish to send you
I'm from heaven
May I visit you
Wishing upon a star
I found a wishing well
I'll cheer you up
Squeeze my hands
I'm your friend
The little flower sent me to you
Angels are up above
A wish of yours
Is under the Christmas tree
Sometime soon
Maybe tomorrow
My name
Archangel raphael
What is an archangel

Might you ask
A loved, soldier of a man
Not known
A very complicated story
Of
Jesus Joseph and Mary
I'm powerful
And love you so
Never forget me, I'll be sad
,

the little flower—a friend of Jesus, she lives in a sandcastle Up
in heaven I met her sometime ago Just a dolly In a wool coat

Heaven, made up of sandcastles and treasures and gems, asleep
I thought There playing in my head angels Angels of heavenly
scent Call upon them They appear Angels from heaven I'll
make a wish, Blow me a kiss From time to time Angels are
from heaven Might I say My name, archangel Raphael

Talk to me from time to time
I truly care
No more tears
I care,

Love Tina — I've traveled in heaven,

Under the ever tree

Dear archangels from heaven

I hate Satan; all people that love the devil; destroy them
Until the abyss is filled, Devil and assistants were released,
archangels take position And send them back to the abyss,

The love of the little flower to avail on my finger,

Closures;

The obnoxious bitch,

The love of st Michael
I adore you
Your legs
The demons attack destroy
Capturing a moment or moments

In time
I dare not recover
The life of st Jude
The garland of roses
Standing by the door
St Raphael are you there
There is no mercy
When the unnamed is touch
A war between darkness
And light
There to recover
The medal of the Maddonna
I thought I love you

A classic moment of the demonic plague of hearing voices

This is a moment captured by a friends influence,

Uriel and valentine

Valentine, I have you

Jattidles, raisins kattodles

Oh Mary, I love you ever.
The promises of her rosary, such beauty in her vail; "god,
does abandon a servant of the virgin,,; all found in her rosary;
Though, i can't recite her prayer the gem i digested; Just the
same as saying the gem; Knees on the floor, All seriousness, I love
you ever virgin, my life I owe you as writer For your rosary,

Black lace and burgundy roses, valentine and uriel

Dearest Marium,

Ever virgin, valentine and Uriel,

Valentine and little flower, it is January 31st, 2014

Looking at your vail, past writing; "can't believe what
two years ago to now is.—jattidles and on the silent
typewriter Gold of jeers to valentine and flower

Both of you fell in love
Jesus and little flower
Was it the vail of the Maddonna
Or the mystery of thorns against a naked body Such beauty in
ureil being the body parts of a woman Then again Woman is
not a name Just just say tears of gold Such boring words.
Roses are a thing of the past
Uriel is now my breast
and body and everything
Demons chat valentine as I tap tap
Of words of gold
A preprogramed brain
Oh gosh
I wish the nudity would return
(said in sultry seductive tone)
Two lovers in the garden
Thorns and burgundy roses
Oh valentine
The sexy of a figure
black and burgundy lace

(the brain activity; not hearing rhythm in
the voices) January 31st, 2014

Pitter patter if the keyboard
Such a boring life of the voices (demonic control) Just chats in
gold, the virgin And her crown I adore Mary, I prefer calling you
Marium Staring at you in black and white Images and sounds
of perfume Violin and piano Nudity is a beautiful thing

(one would say, in orgasm chic
The words, nipples are as raisins, just laughter I
await on Mary Garland of roses beneath my feet
Garden of thorns and burgundy roses Beneath

Raisins for her nipples, apples for her breasts
Valentine takes a bite

The laughter of Uriel
To valentine
Oh valentine
Must you be a tease,

Scratches from valentine
On my apples
Love bites from you valentine

Thorns and burgundy roses
Burgundy roses just burgundy roses
Sun and rain never sets in
Nudity in the garden
Valentine visit me again

I hate Satan, archangel michael,
Theres wicked in words of gold
Perfume from the virgin and her vail

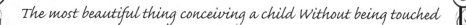

The most beautiful thing conceiving a child Without being touched

Mary I adore you so,

I must tell you, unexplainable touches Nothing in comparison For
josephs love for you And the archangel Gabriel whispering in my ear

Messages from valentine
Nudity in the garden
Yet there's no fear

I must not curse, then again
In the heated moment
Oh touch me touch me
Don't stop
Such boring words,

Valentine, oh valentine
I ll wait for valentine,
Archangels that are from heaven defeat Satan,

Valentine being distracted from you
I can't no more
Just burgundy roses
Nudity, and leaves

Unexplainable touches
I haven't felt
Marium and her gem

Bowing in the garden, I'm a good girl; unnamed Holding her gem, Mary's promise, god would never punish anyone faithful To the rosary; my name is Mary, for everything Mary is going to do for me Just valentine and love bites Mary, a part of untouchable feelings

Love story of Tmj 2014

The promises of the rosary, Marium, since the Maddonna is out ready For publication; your writer and servant; is awaiting your promises On her everything, I now call the rosary, your gem, your saints and archangels Jeerful in their ever tree and garland of roses, leave me never Oh Marium; just a brain thing; your name now Marium; I love the new me, past life some of past life just past life. (words are gold, Mary, thoughts after a Demons attempt destruction, in a journey.) childish twang (Mary destroy for me, I am a writer from the archangels and you) sandcastle village, Oh archangels, I need my writing, creativity and everythingbas Satan attempted to have me confused as a friend of his, st Jude This must not be, attack without death; for the writer and servant I am of heaven

Tina Mary Jesus, writer for heaven, 2014

Archangels and saints from heaven, the books
are almost published, my words.
Of jeers for heaven). visit all the people that sends curses
and spells Torture them with tears for centuries, truly
finding you, St Gabriel; my heart is devout to heaven,

A love letter to the virgin Mary

Orgasm chic becomes quiet
Wants to taught
The devil robbed her of her brain
The virgin rescued
Her through
Prayer
All in the brain, though the sensation was real,

She didn't have sex with anyone.

The life with the virgin
And working for her
The archangels made the difference

I'm a lover of the Islamic princess

A new life after marrying
Archangel Michael
The terror of the devil,

Xx xx xx xx